A Thousand Years of
Social & Economic History
in DARSHAM

by

Richard Ginn, Olive Reeve
&
Andrew Campbell

MMVIII

Published by
The Darsham Parochial Church Council

Sold in aid of All Saints' Church Fabric Fund

ISBN No: 978-0-9536592-1-0

Acknowledgments:

British Library
University of East Anglia library
Essex Record Office
Norfolk Record Office
Suffolk Record Office
The National Archive, Kew
Suffolk Library Service
Times Newspapers Ltd
East Anglian Daily Times
& Eastern Counties Newspapers Ltd.
Darsham Parochial Church Council

Printed by: Leiston Press, Unit 1b, Masterlord Industrial Park,
Leiston, Suffolk. IP16 4JD

Cover Photos: *The Low Road and The Parish Church - c.1905*

CONTENTS

Introduction 1

Ch 1 - Domesday to Doomsday 3

Ch 2 - From Bad to Worse 12

Ch 3 - All Parcelled out: All Stitched up 19

Ch 4 - The Sixteenth Century - Change & Change About......... 27

Ch 5 - The Miseries of England - Darsham & the National Turmoil 1600 - 1660 37

Ch 6 - The beginnings of Stability 1660 - 1760 47

Ch 7 - Darsham fell off the map! 1761 - 1837 57

Ch 8 - Darsham back on the map! 1837 - 1914 73

Ch 9 - Keeping Sight of Humanity 1914 - 2000 91

Conclusion 105

INTRODUCTION

The verse of the Hymn 'O God, our help in ages past' inspired the title for our Millennium book about a thousand years of the church in Darsham:—

'A thousand ages in thy sight
Are like an evening gone,
Short as ***the watch that ends the night***
Before the rising sun.'

We were very grateful that 'An Evening Gone' was so well received.

After we had recovered from that book we realised that there was still a huge amount of material on the social and economic history of Darsham that we had not touched. So we began to dream of a sequel to 'An Evening Gone' and so naturally turned to the words 'The Watch that Ends the Night.' We felt that we had kept watch over history and that the result of our short watch might dispel some of the darkness — the night that shrouds our history — and that light might be revealed.

Whilst so much of our history is unrecorded and lost, enough survives to tell a connected story that illustrates the struggles of a thousand years. We have been surprised at the information that has been preserved — particularly about the tax records which go back to the Middle Ages. We may throw tax papers away after 7 years — it seems that the government keeps records for centuries!

We hope that this book will be patronised as well as the last — and that it will enable people to feel affection for our ancient Parish of Darsham. Every place has a story, and we hope that these pages about Darsham might also encourage others to cherish and research the places which are special to them.

Chapter One

Domesday to Doomsday

The freezing winter storms of 1047 killed men and cattle, birds and fishes. There was a period of cold wet summers and frosty winters that lasted from about 1000 until the middle of the twelfth century in 1150. The severe weather of 1042 had blighted crops and killed cattle. In 1044 there had been widespread famine. A millennium ago the weather had immense impact on early English settlements, and a necessary part of any introduction to life at this time is to talk about the weather. These were miserable times for ordinary people. Most lived in tiny isolated communities. At Darsham there would have been perhaps two households beside the manor, with land held communally.

From a wider perspective things looked different. The country seemed to have potential enough for William of Normandy to consider that conquest was desirable.

Compilation of the Domesday Book in 1086 was the direct result of the Norman Conquest. Its name arose from its authority in judgement (old English: dóm) on the matters contained in it. The first detailed record of life in Darsham is thus written down. The primary purpose of the Domesday Book had been to record the assets and income of the (new) tenants-in-chief from their lands. Many details were omitted, none-the-less the Domesday entries for Darsham reflect the reality of conquest and subjugation for the few poor families living there.

In 1086, a generation after the Conquest, the principal landowners for Darsham were King William; Roger Bigot, one of William's fellow countrymen and now Sheriff of Norfolk & Suffolk; Count Alan of Brittany who was son-in-law to William; and Esilia, Robert Bigot's mother, widow of William Mallet who had fought alongside William at Hastings. Anskitel the priest held the manor. He was the chaplain of Roger Bigot. It is worth noting too that Roger Bigot's family, the future Earls of Norfolk, was soon to found Thetford Priory which figures large in the history of Darsham in the middle-ages.

The Domesday Book distinguishes between how land was held before 1066, and how it was held in 1086. So we know that the lands of Anskitel had formerly been held by free-men, and even a free-woman. Before the conquest there had been two bordars (labouring cottagers with little or no land), but in 1086 there were 11 bordars. These numbers may seem small, but in a population of less than 50 adults, this was a dramatic transformation. Over the period of a single generation, a free 'frontier society' had been regularised and regulated with a new pattern of civil structure that was to pave the way for the monastic domination of the middle ages.

Suffolk was comparatively a developed area of the country, with an agricultural tradition going back to Roman times. Despite the weather, and despite the conquest, there were still signs of prosperity as revealed by the Domesday information about plough-teams. A plough-team consisted of eight oxen, who would be worked in pairs. Before the conquest the Manor held half a plough-team (i.e. four oxen), and by 1086 this had increased to a whole plough-team. Meanwhile, there were also two plough-teams belonging to the men. So by 1086 there were two dozen working oxen in Darsham - a valuable source of motive power and manure. The fact that the men of the village retained their oxen indicates that whilst the land had come under Norman control, the men retained rights over the means of agricultural production. They may have lost their land, but the land was useless without their labour, and the slow and steady tramp of their oxen.

Ansketil's income from his holding was reckoned at twenty-five shillings a year. Perhaps that does not sound very much until it is compared with the price of a plough-team - which was one pound. A plough-team then was the equivalent of a large tractor today - except that oxen ate local produce rather than diesel, gave out milk and manure rather than exhaust fumes, reproduced without recourse to the sales staff of Massey-Fergusson or John Brown, and at death became a valuable source of food and raw materials. Strangely, there was no mention of sheep in the Domesday entry for Darsham. The principal crop was most probably barley.

Barley would have been used for bread and for malt, thus providing the staple foods of bread and weak beer.

The modern popular view of life in mediaeval England has been romanticised — actually life was really hard. In addition to the pressure of the upper layers of society who expected the co-operation and work of the virtually enslaved 'bordars,' there was the weather (and the mud), and the reality of under-nourishment. It has been calculated that twelve acres of land were necessary at the time of Domesday to feed two adults and two to three children. Agricultural yields were low, for example the barley grown at that time was a primitive low yielding crop. Modern Darsham has about 1200 acres under cultivation. Ansketil was credited with holding 120 'fiscal' acres: indicating their notional value for the purposes of assessment. The implication is that there was enough land under cultivation for ten families, but Ansketil could call on the services of eleven bordars, which implies eleven families, plus various other local residents. The reality was that hunger was normal, there was only low resistance to disease and life was short.

There had been the Norman Conquest of 1066, and then the way of life in Darsham was changed again around 1107 when the manor of Darsham became part of the foundation endowment of Thetford Priory. Now Darsham became part of the monastic system and a source of income to a distant priory. The relentless pressure of a system that was supposed to generate 25 shillings a year out of the poverty of an oppressed people now became geared to a larger enterprise.

Mercifully for the people of Darsham the weather improved, and it is no co-incidence that the end of the cold years (approximately 1150) marks the time to which the first phase of the re-building of the parish church has been attributed. The new life of the countryside eased the pressure on the population as agricultural productivity increased, and the accelerating revenues of Thetford Priory released funds, materials and man-power for the building of the central core of Darsham Church as it is seen today, roughly from the main door to the priest's door, and to a height of about three quarters of the present walls. Whilst this work would have taken many years, it would have been impossible without an improved climate allowing the mortar in the walls to dry out and stabilise.

1150 is a good marking point in the local history of our part of Suffolk. The improving climate was linked to a rising population — which meant that more land began to be cultivated — which further meant that the pattern of monastic land control was gradually extended.

So it was that about 1150 Sibton Abbey was founded by William de Casineto, also known as William Cheney. The name of 'Cheney' was associated with the western end of the village of Darsham for centuries. The Cheney family gave land in Darsham to Blythburgh Priory and Leiston Abbey.

The hard earned wealth of Darsham also came to be committed to regular outflows to Sibton Abbey and the Priory of Horsham St. Faith in Norfolk. By 1290 these dues were fixed. Thetford Priory was receiving the great tithe worth 15 marks (£10) per year, the vicar received the small tithe worth 6½ marks (£4: 6s: 8d) per year and the Priory of Horsham St Faith received 30 shillings (£1: 10s: 0d). These onerous figures constituted the basis of ecclesiastical assessment for the next quarter of a millennium.

Whether ecclesiastical dues were to be paid in cash or kind can have made little difference. The sums were an annual 'first call' on the people of Darsham until the Dissolution of the Monasteries. The taxes of the State were extra. The effect of oppressive taxation meant that there was no possibility for wealth accumulation among the mass of the peasantry, but for the monastic foundations the effect was somewhat different. In order to see what resulted from the colossal income received by Thetford Priory the modern citizen of Darsham should make an effort to go to see the Thornham Parva Retable which is said to have been the reredos of the high altar of Thetford Priory. The implication is that the glories of the monastic system were founded on the endless struggles of the poor. In bad years they were locked into a system from which there was no escape; in better years they may have been glad to consecrate the sweat of their labours by such dues, but it is an inescapable fact that the worthy monastic vows of poverty and obedience were felt to a

The remains of Thetford Abbey
founded in 1104
by Roget Bigot
which features in the early history of Darsham

The remains of Sibton Abbey
founded c.1150 by Wm. de Casineto
Also known as Wm Cheney

much greater extent outside the walls of the local monastery.

Amongst the papers surviving from the Middle Ages is a Cartulary of Blythburgh Priory. This volume is now in the British Library [ADD MS 40725]. The collection was owned by the Rector of Thorington in 1885, evidently remaining close to its place of origin. Included in the recitation of rights and properties of Blythburgh Priory is the *'Customary of the Men of Hinton'* — setting out the contractual relations between the prior and the men of Hinton, as agreed about 1250. Hinton is close to Darsham. Can this agreement be taken as a parallel to the expectations clustered around the populace of Darsham?

The men of Hinton had to plough the prior's lands. They had to use their own ploughs. Such ploughs would almost certainly have been made of wood and would have had a short life. The prior at Blythburgh would do well to avoid the added expense of having ploughs made continually for the tilling of his lands. In any case, if men had to use their own ploughs they would take better care of them. Through the winter and spring they had to give one morning's work per week, and during June and July this extended to one whole day. They had to reap four days per week during the autumn (note the later date of harvest and the effect that would be likely to have on yield in poor weather conditions), and cart corn. In the winter they had to cart dung. Carting dung, mowing meadows, digging turves and shearing sheep would be rewarded with a meal. "At the Feast of St. Andrew (30th November) they shall each give three chickens, and they shall dine with the convent." They had to pay fixed rates for their oxen, calves, cows, sheep. The meal at the priory for the men of Hinton consisted of eight loaves and "beer of the second quality". Thus rights and duties were spelt out, and in this kind of pattern the local economy turned on its way.

Between 1250 and 1350 there are records nationally of new field systems, new crop rotations, the use of marling and liming, and the introduction of many different drainage techniques. Barley yields were mostly between three and fourfold, in other words one seed of barley yielded three or four seeds at harvest. Population numbers rose, but this meant no scarcity of labour, which in itself played into the hands of the local monastic authorities. The peasantry had no basis for negotiation to secure a better deal.

In spite of increased crop yields, the margins between sufficient harvest and scarcity were very narrow. Grain prices could see-saw wildly, and natural disaster and fatal illness were close at hand. The great storm of 1286, which caused the decline of nearby Dunwich as a port, was one sign of the vulnerability of mediaeval society. The watershed of the Black Death extinguished the relative prosperity that had developed by the mid-1300s in a different way.

Chapter Two

From Bad to Worse

Successive waves of plague carried off perhaps one half of the population of Europe. In 1349, in Norwich alone, some 60,000 people were said to have perished. The Archbishop of Canterbury died of the plague at this time, as did two vicars at Darsham. In broadest terms the Black Death, as these particular outbreaks of the plague were called, meant that the country swung from not being able to produce enough food to not having enough people to produce food. However, as well as considering the effects of the plague, more light can be thrown on this period in the history of Darsham by looking at the influence of three factors: the population surplus before the plague struck; people therefore having to move around to find work; the effects of the renting out of monastic land, and a factor that was eventually to lead to open rebellion: government taxation.

The so-called Subsidy Return for Darsham for the year 1327 has survived. Examining these records helps us to complete the picture of the way the inhabitants of Darsham were taxed before and during the time when the Black Death ravaged the population at large.

The Subsidy Return contains a list of more than forty

Darsham people who had to pay taxes on moveable goods. This form of tax was one that the government often resorted to, and it was usually imposed in country districts at the rate of one fifteenth on the assessed value. For Darsham, even the amount paid by individual residents has been recorded. We can see the proportion of the population that consisted of migrant workers, because those who had originated from outside the parish also had their native place recorded as a surname. Not all these places are recognisable, though the following will be familiar: Norwico, Glemham, Stonham, Donewys and Sylham, but what about Johanne Therrich? Is this a nickname, 'John the Rich'? — not one to be known of by greedy authorities! Or what about 'Henrico le Eyr': a government spy? However the following are probably self evident: Johanne le Tannour, Johanne le gardiner and Johanne de Norwico-Clerico. More seriously, the total bill inflicted on these villagers for this particular tax in 1327 came to £3.18s 2d., individual bills ranging from three pence up to five shillings.

In 1349, the first full year of the Black Death, the King declared a freeze on wages and prices. In 1351 when parliament was once again able to meet following the first outbreak of the plague this became the Statute of Labourers. The annual wage for certain classes of labourer was set. For example, a swineherd was to receive six shillings per year, a plough driver seven shillings. This shows the Subsidy Return to have been a gruelling imposition in Darsham, worth maybe the income of ten sturdy men. Looking at this tax from another point of view, it implies that the assets of the whole village were worth less than £60, and the village was already committed to the Ecclesiastical Tithe totalling £15. 16s 8d., though at least this tithe was linked to income. The subsidy return functioned as a property tax and that made it doubly unwelcome.

As well as the record for the Subsidy Return of 1327, the 'Nonarium Inquisitiones' of 1340/41 has also survived for Darsham. The government was desperate to finance its wars and so had continuously to raise money through taxation. The idea of this tax was that after the tithe (tenth) had been paid to the Church, then a ninth of what was left would be paid to the Crown. The ninth was assessed on the production of corn, lambs, and wool and was calculated for Darsham to be £7. 6s 8d. The return for Darsham was attested by four local men, who included 'Henry Le Eyr' and 'Johan de Sylham' — names which had been listed as Taxpayers in 1327. The laconic records of this 'Inquisition of the Ninth' record a village that was working hard before the plague came to carry away its shreds of happiness. Flax and hemp were producing valuable crops, and milk and veal were important.

It was the population surplus which lead to localised overcrowding, and this helped the spread of the plague,

Raising Money through Taxation
to Finance the Wars

DERSH'M.

Ext' xv m̃r'.

Vicar' vj m̃r' & di'.

Por° s̃te Fid' xxx^s.

It̃ dic' q̃d nona garb̃ vell̃ & agnoƺ eccl̃ie de Dersham val' vij^li vj^s viij^d Et nõ plus q, sunt ibid̃m xxx acr' t̃re de dote eccl̃ie que val' xxx^s It̃ ij acr' prat' que val' iij^s iiij^d It̃ decim' fen' que val' xx^s It̃ obl' p iij dies p̃ncipal' & al' minut' decim' dict' eccl̃ie ptinent' val' xlvij^s It̃ decim' lin' & canab' val' xx^s It̃ decim' lact' & vitloƺ val' L^s Ut testat̃ p William Marrote Henr' Eyr Henr' Hyllek Johẽm de Sylham pochin' eccl̃ie p̃dict' cor' dc̃o abb̃e & soc' suis jur'.

The Nonarium Inquisitiones of 1340/41
Listing the names of Darsham taxpayers
and the payments due

SUBSIDY RETURN - DARSHAM - 1327

	s.	d.
Adam de Sullington	v.	
Johanne de Norwico - Clerico	iii.	
Willimo Ams		xii.
Rogero de Glemham	iii.	
Johanne Lylie		vi.
Johanne Therrich	iii.	vi.
Adam Lylie		vi.
Adam Filio Johannis	ii.	
Henrico Coco		x.
Johanne Moryel	ii.	
Ricardo Kanne		xii.
Galfido le Neue	v.	
Andrea Styward		xviii.
Adam Harre		xii.
Johanne Baldry		vi.
Johanne Seer		vi.
Roberto Wolfard		vi.
Roberto de Stonham		vi.
Willmo Michel	iii.	vi
Henrico le Eyr	iii.	vi.
Alexandro de Donewys	iii.	
Johanne le Tannour	ii.	
Galfrido Ode		x.
Willmo Cockok	ii.	vi.
Johanne de Sylham		xviii.
Johanne le Provost		xviii.
Johanne le Gardiner		xii.
Willmo Pentel	ii.	iii.
Alicia Edeth		xviii.
Rogero de Prato		x.
Waltero Fabro		x.
Elia Preposito		x.
Willmo del Hil		x.
Johanne Theny (Cheny?)		viii.
Johanne Deree		viii.
Rogero Gos		vi.
Willmo Kyng		ix.
Johanne Wryne		x.
Willmo Serjaunt		iii.
Ricardo Elyanor		iii.
Willmo Heylok		iii.
Willmo Margarete		iii. = Summa = Lxxviii. ii.

but as well as this it had its effect on the land used for growing food. Soils were to become exhausted leading to an undernourished population through failure of crops. In the years before the Black Death marginal land, where the soil was poor, was already being abandoned as being no longer viable for crop production. The monasteries held much agricultural land. They found that they could secure a more stable income by renting out their land rather than trying to farm it in their own right. The tenants were having to pay rent on land which was becoming less and less productive. On the other hand the landless poor presented another problem. These were people who were desperate for food, work and shelter. Lawlessness was on the increase. Lembaldes, or Lymballs Farm to give it its modern name, has a moat. Is this an example of moat construction commonly associated with isolated manor houses from the period 1275 - 1325 when such moats were constructed for protection against such poor and desperate individuals?

The picture of farming in Darsham in these years has to be built from tantalising snippets of information. There would have been varying practice between manors (farmed by their owners with labour provided by tenants), tenanted and common land. A likely rotation of cropping ran to the following sequence: (1) fallow; (2) wheat or barley; (3) oats, dredge (oats & barley mixed together), or peas.

Sheep herding aimed to achieve one lamb per ewe each year. The ratio of rams to ewes was one ram to thirty or forty ewes, but there were huge variations in practice and achievement. Sheep were grazed on open pasture during the day, but between harvest and ploughing they were penned at night with hurdles on particular pieces of arable land, so that landlords could ensure their tenants' land was manured. This activity was subject to considerable control. Apart from wool, sheep were vital to the agricultural economy for their contribution to soil fertility. Sheep were vulnerable to a plague-like disease, which was loosely described as murrain. Murrains occurred often locally, and the records of Sibton Abbey show murrains occurring in 1363, 1365 & 1372. About one third of their flock died on each occasion. It is quite likely that Darsham was affected by such episodes.

Both horses and oxen could be used for ploughing, but ploughing was very expensive, both because of the cost of the plough, and the slow speed of work. Ploughing teams on heavy land in Suffolk were recorded as combining four horses and four oxen, or six horses and two oxen.

Rabbits had occurred in England since the Norman invasion. They breed more readily than sheep, and by the fourteenth century they were beginning to achieve commercial significance. They could be worth 2½d or 3d each. Their meat was a luxury and their fur was used for warm clothing, bed coverings and for making into hats — essential wear in the worsening climate. Swans may not have been part of the Darsham economy, but they were usually worth 3 shillings each.

Weather patterns were changing during the fourteenth century. The climate cooled so that the production of English wine ceased. Some selected examples of general facts concerning effects of weather and the prevalence of disease make a sad list:

1315 – 1316	Harvest failure
1313 – 1317	Sheep Murrain
1319 – 1321	Cattle Murrain
1348 – 1351	The Black Death
1356	The Black Death
1361 – 1362	The Black Death
1368 – 1369	The Black Death
1370	Famine

It was the effects of taxation on a desperate populace which brought the country to open rebellion. The 1377 Poll Tax was levied on all persons over 14 years of age, and that of 1381 on all persons over the age of 15 years. The overall figures for Suffolk for those who paid the Poll Tax exists as follows:

	1377	1381
Suffolk	58,610	44,635
Ipswich	1,506	963
Bury St. Edmunds	2,445	1,334

The seeming fall in figures for the population over a four year period demonstrates the evaporation of the fiscal population. In 1381 people quite simply left their dwellings and even went and lived in the woods and fields to escape the tax. The appointments of special commissioners to search out missing tax payers only inflamed the population. There was already widespread anger at efforts to enforce the Statute of Labourers (as well as fixing wages for labourers the statute forbade the giving of alms to sturdy beggars). So it was that hatred of the Poll Tax focussed discontent, and what followed was the rising know as The Peasants' Revolt.

At Bury St. Edmunds the abbot and some of the monks were executed. Strife here was fuelled by the long-standing disregard by the Abbey for the struggle for survival of the surrounding inhabitants. The Archbishop of Canterbury was also murdered, and in many places estate registers were seized and burnt by a furious populace, anxious to rid itself of the impossible burden of customary obligation.

Chapter Three

"All parcelled out: all stitched up!"

In writing about the 15th Century, it would be foolish to imagine that one could conjure up an encomium of "Merrie England." There had been the terror of the plague and the chaos of the insurrection. So it was not surprising that 'death and control' became characteristic preoccupations of the years to follow.

This new era really began in the year 1388 when Parliament met in Cambridge. The law called 'The Statute of Cambridge' was a new poor law that introduced new principles into English life. These principles have been said to have continued in essence until 1929.

The first principle was to make a distinction between the 'sturdy beggars' capable of work and beggars who were incapacitated by illness or by advancing years. The second principle was that servants were forbidden to move out of their Hundred without carrying formal legal permission. The Hundred was an administration division of the county, (also known in East Anglia as a Leet) originally composed of a hundred families. These Hundreds gradually diminished in importance after the mid-1800s, until the Local Government Acts of 1888-

1894 set up County, District & Parish Councils. So in Mediaeval times, people could travel on their master's business, but could not move any distance. Whilst each Hundred was responsible for housing and keeping alive their own paupers no provision was made for the sick poor. For more than two centuries to come, only charity could safeguard the old and infirm against starvation or against simply freezing to death.

Another feature of this act of 1388 was that the process of enforcement was entrusted to the Justices of the Peace. From 1388 until the Poor Law Amendment Act of 1834, Justices of the Peace administered the Poor Law — bringing the weight of the authority of the Crown directly to bear in a system which could be accused of imprisoning people in their own misery. The small numbers of Justices of the Peace in these years, however, probably meant that the system functioned as a deterrent rather than as an effective control. So life in Darsham may not have been marked by unrelenting oppression.

Village life varied between villages where gentry resided and those that were free of gentry. There were plenty of villages where no gentry lived, simply because there was not enough gentry to go round. Where there were no gentry there is the implication that the villages were more free and more humane places. Even so gentry living at a distance could still have sizeable interest in Darsham. A grant by Henry IV of 23rd October, 1408, confirmed Sir

Roger de Swyllington (the imagination boggles as to what his popular nickname might have been) in holding a charter of free warren in many places, including Darsham (Suffolk R.O. Ref: HA30/312/1) The Swyllington family was based in Swyllington in the West Riding of Yorkshire, six miles south-east of Leeds. This grant confirmed an earlier grant of a charter of free warren in respect of Darsham given to John de Vaux in 1248. It is worth explaining what factors may have awakened Sir Roger de Swyllington's appetite for the rabbits of Darsham in 1408. During the Middle Ages, hunting was carefully regulated. The Monarch held the sole privilege of hunting in the royal forests, but beyond these the Crown was prepared to sell certain exclusive hunting rights for a specific area by means of a charter of free warren. The beasts of warren were the hare, the partridge, the pheasant and the rabbit. The owner of free warren had the exclusive right to keep and to kill rabbits.

Rabbits in those days had not fully adapted to the English climate since their introduction by the Normans and did not breed as recklessly as their modern descendants. Rabbits were valuable for their meat and their fur. Around 1250, when John de Vaux bought the free warren of Darsham, rabbits were priced at 3½d each but even though the price held up after 1300 until the Black Death, the numbers of rabbits available collapsed under the strain of the weather. Numbers of rabbits began to pick up after 1360. Rabbits were still worth 2½d. The price had dropped to 2d by 1400, but the numbers of rabbits had increased vastly. There were probably enough rabbits loose in Darsham for Sir Roger to go to the expense of seeking to have the charter of free warren that had come to him confirmed by the King. Rabbits prefer light soils, but some would have escaped from neighbouring parishes. They may even have been helped to escape. They were certainly subject to organised poaching by armed gangs as well as by respectable people. For example, three monks from Blythburgh were caught poaching rabbits near Dunwich in 1442, using their own trained greyhounds! (Suffolk R.O.Ref: HA30/312/195) However, to read the rights of free warren back into the history of Darsham since 1248 is to see another cause of social pressure — if Darsham residents were caught poaching or with dead animals or the remains of dead animals, they were subject to the Manorial Courts. They could look at this food, even in times of scarcity, but they had no permission to harvest it.

This perception fuelled resentment of feudal privilege and was another factor in the 1381 Peasants' Revolt. This grievance was still being cited in Kett's rebellion in Norfolk in 1549.

Another document, held in London, is dated around 1436. It records that William de la Pole, Earl of Suffolk, gave his land and rents in Darsham "to the master and chaplains of the chantry founded by Eleanor, late wife of

John Wyngefeld, knight in the church of Wingfield." (The National Archives Ref: C143/448/5). Thus the earl's slice of the rewards of the labour of the people of Darsham was diverted to pay for distant chantry priests to seek to secure the repose of the soul of the earl when dead, and the souls of his family. But the earl was living by the fashions of the time, and the more wealthy perceived death as more terrible. As one anonymous poem of the fifteenth century advised:

> Remember that thou shall dye,
> For this world in certentee
> Hath nothyng save deth truele.
> Therefore yn thy mynde use this lessone:
> Liffe so that deth take the yn sesone,

A preoccupation with death may have been part of the adjustment of society as the old order passed away. Times were changing as the influence of the monasteries declined, but this piece of information about the wishes of the Earl of Suffolk demonstrates that the rents of the tenanted population of Darsham at this time still found their way to the monastic houses for one reason or another. The master and chaplain at Wingfield may even have been paid with a supply of cheese. Certainly at this time the Thetford Priory accounts record that Darsham farmers were supplying large quantities of cheese to that priory, the cost of which was often allowed against rent. However concerted rent strikes were becoming more common across the country, and the mechanisms for extracting rents and dues became more feeble.

Colossal disquiet arose around 1450 following the introduction of a new income tax. The King was Henry VI, and his principal minster was William de la Pole, now the Duke of Suffolk. William was widely credited with systematic official corruption and even with responsibility for the death in 1447 of Humphrey, Duke of Gloucester, the King's uncle and heir. In order to save this William, who was also blamed for the disasters of the wars with France, accused of High Treason and facing impeachment in Parliament in 1450, the King decreed his exile for 5 years. But in May of that year, some English sailors took William in hand as he fled abroad. They executed him and threw his body ashore on Dover sands.

It is perhaps a great irony that the labour of the people of Darsham should have been harnessed to fund the prayers for the eternal rest of such a disgraceful individual. One cannot but suspect that his death may have contributed to a lack of enthusiasm for the rendering of the rents from his former lands.

Survival was more pressing. The plague, dominant in the second half of the 15th century, was of great concern. The 'Sweating Sickness' was loose in 1485; to be followed by 'Spanish Pox' in 1498 which so affected its

The Tower
of
All Saints' Church
Darsham

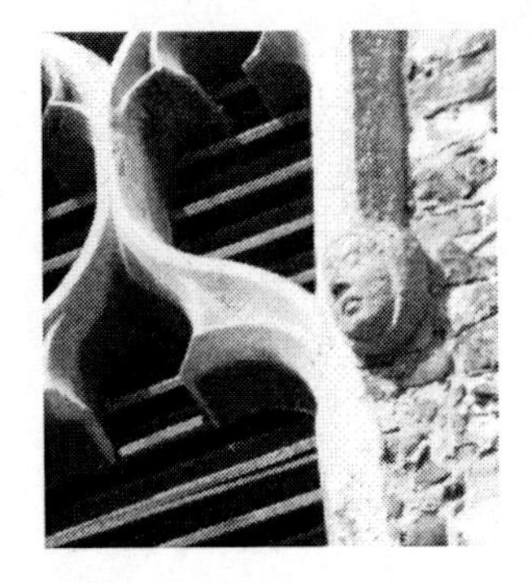

Some of
the gargoyles
on
Darsham Church
Tower

victims that they took two years to recover. And then the plague came again in 1500 to round off the century.

In spite of such hardships there was enough wealth in Darsham to bequeath funds for the building of the church tower between 1460 and 1505. Perhaps there was an element of triumph in the achievement of building the tower — because it meant that nobody else had got their hands on the money! It would be worth savouring the possibility that the gargoyles high up on either side of the bell louvres were contemporary caricatures of the Prior of Blythburgh on the North side, the Abbot of Sibton on the west side, the Abbot of Dunwich to the east, and the Abbot of Leiston on the south — but that might be too convenient an explanation for their appearance! However, gargoyles nearly always depicted local people, who also might have been churchwardens, or those who worked on the building of the church. As a legacy from those difficult times, the tower is a magnificent memorial.

As well as Darsham Church tower there is other evidence of cultural efflorescence during those hard times. One piece of evidence is the so-called "Yoxford Fragment" (Suffolk R.O. Ref: HA30:50/22/13:15). The Yoxford Fragment consists of sheets of music forming the fly-leaves of a description prepared in 1471-2 of the local manors held in and around Yoxford by John Hopton of Cockfield Hall. This music is evidence of local culture. The fact that it could be treated as parchment for recycling in the binding means that it had probably been overtaken by a more current musical taste, so there may have been a musical culture strong enough to survive over a period of more than one generation.

The other piece of evidence also comes from a neighbouring parish — that of Thorington. The account book of Henry Chesham, the churchwarden of Thorington, has survived (Essex R.O. Ref: D/DL E55) from the period 1457-1464 to tell us that fourpence was spent on carriage of an organ, threepence was spent on the binding of a missal, bell ropes were bought, and bellringers were paid. Perhaps they should have been more careful with the organ, because repairing its pipes cost 10 shillings at one point! A rent of 3s 4d still had to be paid to the avaricious absentee landlords, the Swyllingtons, in respect of a property in Wangford. Yet there were books, there were bells and there were priests, there were services, there was music, and there was Darsham church tower. Perhaps a Renaissance was stirring.

Chapter 4

The Sixteenth Century - Change, and Change About

People who live in modern villages expect change, but our mediaeval heritage was that of a society bound by custom and servitude, as well as by oppressive taxation. An ongoing tension developed. On the one hand, there was an assumption that the pattern of village life was lawful because it was what had happened since time immemorial. On the other hand there were pressures of innovation, trade and political power, and economics. This pressure tended to come from further afield. When people write of the Renaissance, they tend to refer to great artists, thinkers and statesmen.

Perhaps the first sign of the dawning of this new age in the locality of Darsham can be taken to be a small item found at Sibton Abbey in 1989. This object has come to be known as the Sibton Abbey Naviculum and it is now in the National Maritime Museum. Basically this was a portable sundial and was called a naviculum because it was in the shape of a boat. It was made about 1450. The size of the palm of a man's hand, most remarkably it was calibrated so that it could be adjusted for use in Exeter, London, Oxford, Northampton and York. The existence of this object gives us a taste of merchant life in the later 15th century. The fact that it was found at Sibton means that our area was part of this new world of trade. This naviculum was accurate to within a quarter of an hour, and bespeaks a world of trade, travel, appointments and profit — a world where time was money.

Such developments meant real change. For a society bound by custom this change was going to be painful. In the offering of faith in the parish church, villagers would regularly hear the words " Sicut erat in principio et nunc et semper" (As it was in the beginning, is now and ever shall be). But those words were of the eternal glory of God, not of the struggles of this world. One of the first of the struggles of this world was the pain of taxation.

Henry VIII went to war with the French. War costs money, and a tax was levied in 1523 called a Subsidy. This was payable over two years, and the list of Darsham residents who paid the tax, how much they paid and on what they were assessed, has survived for 1524.

This subsidy is said to be the first graduated tax. It was levied in a way that meant that those who were wealthier paid more. So it was that Alys Reve, widow of John Reve a farmer, was assessed on goods worth £2, and she had to pay at the rate of 6d in the pound, but John Bukle, gent, had goods worth £30, and he had to pay £1.10s 0d at the rate of 1s in the pound. The total that 27 named residents of Darsham had to pay in 1524 was £6. 3s. 2d.

SUBSIDY RETURN - DARSHAM - 1524

			£ s d
John Bukle - gent	in goodes	£ 30	1. 10. 0.
Simon Gonell	in wages	£ 1	4.
John Broun	in goodes	£ 34	1. 14. 0.
John Reve of Chenies	in goodes	£ 9	4. 6.
William Capon	do	£ 12	6. 0.
Mawte Molett	do	£ 12	6. 0.
Roger Reve	do	£ 7	3. 6.
William Burnham	do	£ 12	6. 0.
John Luff	do	£ 7	3. 6.
John Drane	do	£ 4	2. 0.
Robert Coupe	do	£ 3	1. 6.
Thomas Baldwyn	do	£ 13	6. 6.
Thomas Bonett	do	£ 8	4. 0.
John Reve the yonger	do	£ 5	2. 6.
Thomas Botell	do	£ 3	1. 6.
John Reve - Carpenter	do	£ 2	1. 0.
Robert Fryer	do	£ 3	1. 6.
Alys Reve	do	£ 2	1. 0.
Thomasyn Gonell	do	£ 3	1. 6.
Robert Elyse	do	£ 2	1. 0.
Thomas Melles	do	£ 2	1. 0.
Jaffrey Reve }			
Jaffrey Stannard }			
William Clerk }	£1 each in wages		1. 4.
Henry Reve }			
Roger Mote	in goodes	£ 2	1. 0.
Peter Founten	do	£ 2	1. 0.

	Summa Hujus ville		£6. 3. 2d

The subsidy lists all people over the age of 16 years with an income from land or - with taxable goods worth £2 per year or - with annual wages of £1 or more.

Ref: Suffolk Green Books

Payments of Rents for Land which had been held by Thetford Priory

Arundel Castle Records - Archives of Dukes of Norfolk

Ref: A928   Probable date c.1557-1559

Henry BEDINGFELD 9s;

Robert NORTON gent 10s;

John GEBON 13s 5d;

Robert Reve of Buckles 14s 5d & Meltrons;

Robert REVE of Cheners 41s;

William DURMAN 2s & 3s;

John REVE of Burstell 52s 7d & Nykers 10d & 18s; *1568*

John REVE of Hubbardes 9s 11d;

John REVE of Pynsell 12s;

Robert WALLER per Rowlottes 4d & grete Rowlottes 2s 8d;

Rosa GONELDE widow 18d & 4d;

Oliver DEVE 2s;

Thomas REVE 12s;

Robert WEBSTER 15d;

John PALGRAVE 18d;

Anthony COOKE 6s 1d;

Robert ELLIS 2s 10d;

James BRETONY 21s 3d;

Robert NORMAN 2s;

George SAXMUNDHAM 5s;

John BALDWYN per Wichinghams & Sowters 4s 9d;

William FLEMMYNGE 8s 2d & 2d;

Elizabeth HERVIE 2s 4d;

William REVE of Trattelles 18d;

Margerie BURMAN widow 33s 4d.

By contrast, the total assessment for Yoxford was £6. 8s. 2d, Westylton was set at £5. 2s. 2d, and Sibton (Abbey & Town combined) was £6. 5s 8d. This suggests that Darsham was an equal player with Yoxford and Sibton and that Darsham was by now a prosperous place with many individuals being economically significant.

In this context we can note that John Reve, who farmed at Darsham around the end of the previous century had left four heifers among other items; one to each of his two daughters and the other two elsewhere. The continuing ability to produce milk was perhaps a more sure way of meeting the monastic system of taxation. By the time of the subsidy, payment was to be made with money.

The monastic system as it affected Darsham was in decline. The activities of Thetford Priory were being curtailed in the early 1500s partly because new ventures in trade and manufacture tended to pass them by, but also partly by statute. In 1529 its activities would have been limited to supplying the needs of its own household and guests. The main manor of Darsham, held by Thetford Priory, was probably farmed by the under-tenants, and we find them reacting to economic pressure in the same way as modern farmers have done and diversifying. A man called John Reve is recorded in the Subsidy of 1524 as being primarily a carpenter.

In the 1520's, Suffolk was among the richest counties of

England. This was a century in which the population of London exploded from about 50,000 in 1500 to 200,000 by 1600. However, population growth was not an even progress. Growth was halted again whilst a new killer disease took its toll — this illness was called the 'English Sweat' — and this in an age when the only popular deodorant may have been lavender!

Two more factors made country life more and more difficult. The first factor was inflation and the second factor was that it became increasingly difficult to feed a growing population. The primary food of the poor was bread and the price of grain increased sixfold during the sixteenth century. By the end of the century conditions for the poor had become terrible. Most of the labouring poor earned at least some of their wages in cash, and for some of their work they were paid in kind. The population increase flooded the labour market, so employers could pay less, meanwhile the real value of wages declined erratically from 1500 onwards. By 1625 the purchasing power of a day's pay was one third of what it had been in 1500. The fear of disorder generated the Poor Law Act of 1598 which attempted to ensure that the needs of the poor were met in their parish of origin, thus trying to control the growing mass of wandering landless labourers — the dispossessed and the desperate poor — and anchoring them in their home patch.

Arrangements were made for gathering and distributing a

poor rate in every parish.

The monastic system was brought to an end by statute. In 1540 after the dissolution of the monasteries, the Crown granted the Manor of Darsham cum Yoxford to Thomas Howard, the 3rd Duke of Norfolk. As events turned out this meant that Darsham must have been insulated against all sorts of pressures for another twenty years. The Norfolks were Roman Catholic. In 1547 the 3rd Duke's son Henry, Earl of Surrey, was executed. The Duke of Norfolk languished in the Tower of London until the succession of Mary Tudor to the throne in 1553 and died the following year. A grandson had been born in 1538. He was taken from his mother and placed in a controlled and supervised upbringing. After Thomas Howard, the 3rd Duke's death, the new 4th Duke was still a minor. The lands were held by the Crown during his minority and affairs at Darsham continued as per custom until he came of age in 1559.

Amazingly, details of rents paid by Darsham residents to the Duke of Norfolk's estate just before the Duke turned 21 have been preserved at Arundel Castle. Twenty five individuals are recorded and only four of them paid more than £1 per year. This was the stuff of a commonwealth of unpretentious well-being.

1559 was a watershed; the 4th Duke embraced a lavish

lifestyle and was always anxious for money. He was England's only Duke, and as a territorial magnate, was in a class of his own. He had palaces in Norwich and London, and when he travelled between palaces, he could have an entourage of a hundred mounted riders in livery. So once the 4th Duke could begin to exploit his inheritance, the residents of Darsham became very vulnerable. Not only did Darsham feel the pressure of providing for their Duke. Affairs of state also impinged upon Darsham. Like her father, Elizabeth I needed money, and Parliament granted a subsidy in 1566. The list of those who paid the second part of the subsidy have survived. In 1568 only fifteen individuals in Darsham were assessed liable for the subsidy, and the total expected amounted to £4. 17s. 4d compared with the £6.3s. 2d paid in 1524. Subsidies for the neighbouring Yoxford had shot up to £17. 8s. 0d. This was because of the presence of Sir Owen Hopton at Cockfield Hall. He was recorded as holding lands which produced £160 per year, but was famous as the custodian of Lady Katherine Grey on the orders of Queen Elizabeth I from 1567 to 1568, and became Lieutenant of the Tower of London from 1570 to 1590. He was plainly of significant wealth.

The increasing wealth of Sir Owen was a reflection on the behaviour of the economy of the nation as a whole. It was an era in which the rich could dominate and prosper at the expense of the poor. However in the end the wealth and prestige of the 4th Duke of Norfolk did not protect him against disgrace and execution in 1572. The Crown seized the Norfolk estates and employed two of the Duke's old surveyors, William Dix and William Cantrell to harness the income from the lands. These two gentlemen functioned as patrons at the presentation of a new Vicar of Darsham in 1575.

Darsham was an agricultural parish, and animals featured in seven of the wills from the time of the dissolution of the monasteries (1536) until 1568. These are wills of tenant farmers and they imply a certain prosperity among this group of individuals. Twenty two wills survive from the 16th century. Draught animals do not feature in any other wills outside the period of the middle of the century, which suggests that these animals belonged exclusively to the landowners at the beginning of the century and again by the end of the century. The interlude of prosperity for the ordinary people of Darsham became submerged in changing economic circumstances.

So what of the rich landowning classes? Reference has been made to Sir Owen Hopton at Cockfield Hall — he was a member of a new breed of small scale tycoons, thriving on positional privilege. As Lieutenant of the Tower of London, Hopton had personal charge of the Duke of Norfolk and so ironically, the landowner of Yoxford had the landlord of Darsham under lock and key. However, Darsham had its own local magnate, who was probably introduced as a tenant at Darsham Hall. This was John Wentworth. We know he was wealthy because in 1578 he bought four of the Westleton manors from Sir Owen Hopton for £2,000. John Wentworth is first recorded as being in Darsham in 1571. He had married Elizabeth Southwell of Barham Hall, Suffolk, in 1569, and they established themselves in Darsham where they had three children baptised between 1576 & 1581, and where Elizabeth Wentworth was buried in 1598.

John Wentworth does not seem to have owned land in Darsham. He possibly arrived in Darsham as part of a deliberate strategy to act as a tenant for the Norfolk Estates. Settled Darsham folk became his under-tenants. The gap between the rich and the poor was widening and the poor were the indigenous folk of Darsham.

After 1568, the year of the last will of a 16th century Darsham resident that mentioned animals, the number of wills declined. In the first two thirds of the century, 17 wills were laid down for posterity. In the last third of the century, only 5 wills were left for us. This implies not only that people became poorer in Darsham, but also that people of any substance were abandoning Darsham. There had been a full-time carpenter in Darsham in 1524, such skills tended to be handed on in a customary society.

Where were these people going? Perhaps a clue lies in a key piece of Elizabethan legislation: The Statute of

Artificers of 1563. Under this Act, all males between the ages of 12 and 60 who did not belong to one of a number of specific occupations were regarded as wage labourers. The same Act also set upper wage limits for skilled workers such as butchers or carpenters. The intention was that even though prices might rise, wages would not increase. This meant a drop in standard of living for many workers and, not surprisingly, semi-skilled workers migrated to towns in search of betterment. The poor followed if they could.

It has already been noted that the situation of the poor deteriorated during the century, and towards the end of the century despair intensified. The autumn of 1594 saw the first of a series of four failed harvests. Small farmers could neither feed their families nor pay their rent. Those with more land could feed their dependents but had no surplus for sale and so no income by which to profit from the famine. In 1573, a poor harvest had driven wheat prices up to 26s.3¾d per quarter. In 1597, prices peaked at 92s per quarter. The misery and deprivation for those left in Darsham can only be imagined.

It was a great credit to the Monarch and her ministers that the country did not disintegrate. Part of the shadow of these times was a process known as engrossing. This was simply the amalgamation of small farms to make a more efficient business. In Darsham, this process would have proceeded by default as people left the village. It is unlikely that the people of Darsham benefited from the prosperity associated with sheep. Only one will from 1567, refers to "six good ewes," otherwise none of them mention sheep. Generally the folding of sheep on arable land was the key to success in farming to ensure soil fertility. It could well be that huge flocks of up to a thousand sheep were used for this purpose, but any sheep and their profit in Darsham probably belonged to the Norfolk Estates.

The sixteenth century was an era in which commitment to agricultural improvement was to begin. Attempts were made to improve stocks, plants and soil. Land enclosure would allow dramatic advances in such improvements during the course of the next two centuries. One Suffolk practice that may have been used in Darsham was that pebbles from the beaches were brought inland and burnt and applied to the fields. This would be a primitive form of mineral fertilizer. Perhaps coastal erosion was not entirely the fault of the North Sea!

The main crops typical of our heavy soil were barley, rye and wheat. Smaller crops were oats, peas and vetches. In years of bad harvest, the poor mixed beech nuts and chestnuts into their bread flour to make it go further. Sixteenth century Darsham, having been fairly sheltered until 1559, thereafter suffered the vicissitudes of the times. The result was a village tempered by hardship. Alas, things were to get even worse.

Chapter 5

The Miseries of England
Darsham and the National Turmoil 1600-1660

In 1600, England and Wales had a population of about 4½ million. Of these about ¼ million lived in London, but there was no other community of comparable size. About six English people in seven lived in a village of less than a thousand people. The most common occupation was small-scale farming. The key social unit was the family.

Perhaps we may wonder about the living circumstances of the humble cottagers of these times. It is all very well to write of the rich and to touch the world of polite conversation and servants, but most of our forebears in this village were poor. Well, we have a description of a typical Suffolk cottage from 1618 in which the construction was described as low framed and thatched. The cottager filled "his wide panels (after they were well splinted and bound) with clay or culme enough well tempered, over which it may bee some of more ability, both for warmth, continuance and comelinesse, doe bestowe a cast of haire, lime and sand made into a morter and layed thereon, rough or smooth as the owner pleaseth". (ed. Francis Hervey "Suffolk in the 17th century, by Robert Reyce, 1618." 1902, p.51). An example in Darsham is the house now known as 'Carpe Diem Cottage'. Probably originally thatched, it was one among several properties, owned by the Darsham Town Trust, occupied by three poor families, the rents going towards the upkeep of the church and assistance to the poor of the parish.

Society was a hierarchy, ranging from the nobility down to cottage dwellers and the poor. Some sense of the structure of English society can be gauged from a survey of England in 1633 when there were 122 peers, 26 Bishops, 300 lesser nobles, 1500 - 1800 knights, 7,000 - 9,000 esquires, and 10,000 - 14,000 'mere gentlemen.' This last category were on the fringe of the ruling class and many of them were merchants or academics or held office under the Crown. It was those above the gentlemen who really counted politically.

The 'ruling class' — for that is what it was — was small enough to be close-knit at county level. In some counties, as in Suffolk, a real sense of cohesion developed as families intermarried and found common purpose. It was recorded in 1618 that " The gentry of Suffolk meet often, conversing most familiarly together, which so winneth the goodwill of one another with all the reverent regard of the meaner sort, and true love and unfeigned affection of their neighbours, that if

'Carpe Diem Cottage'
once the property
of Darsham Town Trust

Originally a
double-dweller
housing three families

Showing the Timber
Construction with
clay or culme filling

SHIP MONEY - 1640

In 1634, a tax was levied on all seaports and maritime counties, nominally to raise a fleet for the defence of the country.

The following year, it was extended to all inland towns and counties and Blything Hundred was rated at £773.12 towards the sum of £8,000 charged to the county of Suffolk for the support of a ship of 800 tons, manned by 320 seamen.

In 1636, John Hampden, a gentleman of Buckinghamshire, refused to pay the tax and judgement went against him in the courts. Nevertheless, his resistance roused all England to the sense of danger to her liberties from the King's government, and the tax was repealed in 1640.

DARSHAM
SHIP MONEY RETURNS - 8th March 1640

Bedingfield Dorothy, widow	£2. 10s. 0d
Harte William	£1. 8s. 4d
Browne Robert	£1. 5s. 0d
Wade Richard	7s. 6d
Haddenham William	15s. 0d
Jordan Henry	16s. 8d
Short John	16s. 3d
Pooley Robert	£1. 2s. 6d
Britten James	2s. 6d
Artys Edward	10s. 0d
Toakelove Thomas	8s. 4d
Goodwyn Henry	6s. 3d
Cheston George	13s. 4d
Haywarde Robert	16s. 3d
Bearte John	8s. 9d
Allen Daniel	4s. 2d
Perce Valentyne	6s. 8d
Mollett Richard	4s. 2d
Backler Edmund	4s. 2d
Scott William	10s.10d
Bottwight Richar	1s. 1½d
Newson Robert	1s. 1½d
Beddingfeild Richard	2s. 1d
Mowser George	1s. 1½d
Eager John - Clerke (*Rev.John Eachard - Vicar 1616 - 1647*)	8s. 4d
Pilborough Walter	4s. 4d
Reeve Robert	4s. 2d
Eager John - Clerke	1s. 3d
Brooke Robert - gent.	8s. 4d
Beddingfield Anne	10s. 0d
Backler Ezekiel	13s. 4d
Bishopp John	1s. 8d
Smyth John	10d
Wade Richard	2s. 6d
Goodwyn Henry	2s. 6d
Harte William - gent.	2s. 6d

differences do arise, which are very seldom, such is the great discretion ever tempered with love and kindness among them, that these divisions are soon smothered and appeased." [ed. Francis Hervey, Robert Reyce: Suffolk in the 17th Century; The Breviary of Suffolk 1618 — (1902) p.60]

Whilst this picture may be idealised, it still evokes a way of life in which harmony and mutual respect shaped human relationships. By this time John Wentworth had moved from Darsham to Somerleyton where, as might be predicted from his progress in Darsham, he now owned lands. The Bedingfields were now the owners of the manors in Darsham, united by marriage with the Wentworths, and as a result related to the Barnardistons.

It is not surprising that in the small world of Suffolk in this era that one family should emerge as being particularly significant — a role which fell to the Barnardistons of Kedington. Under their leadership the 'upper classes' of Suffolk were almost entirely united in their support for Parliament in every major political manoeuvre in the especially difficult period of 1640 - 1660.

This was the era of the Civil War, and from this period we have the first words of earlier times from Darsham that can be authenticated. Three sermons of our vicar,

John Eachard, survive in print. The phrase at the heading of this chapter about the 'Miseries of England' comes from his introduction to one of his sermons. Wisely, in the contentions of the time, Vicar Eachard refused to take sides between the factions within Parliament. Instead he prayed for peace.

John Eachard held the degree of M.A. from Trinity College, Cambridge, and arrived as vicar in 1616. He was a member of an extended clerical family which included a vicar of Yoxford and a rector of Dennington. His writings show his zeal for godliness, and other sources reflect the way that he journeyed with his flock. When Charles I had tried to raise money without Parliament and Ship Money was imposed in 1639, the bill for Suffolk came to £8,000, and the assessment for Darsham came to £17. 1s 10½d of which Vicar Eachard was called to pay 8s. 4d. The effects of Ship Money galvanised the nation in an ever-growing tide of resentment against an administration perceived as being increasingly infatuated with its own significance. So it was not surprising to find the leading citizens of Darsham entering their names on the list subscribing to the support of Parliament in 1642. Vicar Eachard contributed £3. 2s 6d in money and plate out of the Darsham total of £53. 7s 0d. It shows a lot about Darsham's attitude in that they refused to pay King Charles £17, but voluntarily paid Parliament £53.

Vicar Eachard did not figure in the Muster Rolls of 1638, but 62 of the men of Darsham were included. The Scots had invaded England in response to Charles I's attempts to impose his will on religious practice north of the border. The Muster Rolls recorded the names of those men between the ages of 16 and 60 and under the rank of baron, who were expected to bear arms in the event of trouble.

The execution of the King and the rise of the Commonwealth brought about moves to reform. Cromwell attempted to abolish church patronage. All marriages during the Commonwealth period were to be civil ceremonies performed by Justices of the Peace. During those eleven years, only two marriages were entered in the Darsham register, probably entered after the Restoration. The number of baptisms recorded declined sharply and no burials were recorded during the whole period, but this can hardly be taken to suggest that there were no births and deaths in the parish.

Sir Thomas Bedingfield, who had been M.P. for Dunwich in 1621 and 1626, retired to his home in Darsham in 1649 after the execution of the King. It was said that he had refused to work for Oliver Cromwell, but his withdrawal from public life was not necessarily out of any Royalist commitment, more likely out of disenchantment with the corrupt process which had led to the King's death. Living in Darsham kept London at a safe distance.

Anne Bedingfield (1560-1641), who is also commemorated in the chancel of the Parish Church, had a very different path in life. Inheriting land from her father in London, she became the landlady of the Red Bull Theatre, in Clerkenwell in London. She married into a recusant (i.e. Roman Catholic) branch of the family, coming to live as a widow with her Protestant cousins in Darsham. Anne had a reputation as an almsgiver which must have given her a special place in the life of Darsham.

Through her theatrical connection, Anne Bedingfield may well have known Shakespeare who died in 1616. Equally, Shakespeare, in his wanderings through the countryside reflected in the interaction of his characters things that he noticed by way of patterns of life.

Reference can usefully be made to one of Shakespeare's comic characters: Constable Dogberry in 'Much Ado About Nothing.' A constable was a member of village society. He had to find a balance between the rules and regulations that poured out from Westminster on the one hand, and the basic tendency for people to do what they wanted on the other. Of course, being illiterate would help this process !

A List of the leading Citizens of Darsham who contributed Money and Plate in Support of Parliament in 1642

"An account of the money and plate in the several townes within the said Hundred formerly subscribed upon the propositions of Parliament". The list includes the money & plate relating to Darsham and ends:
"The total sum of the money and plate subscribed in the Townes and Corporations above sd within the Hundred of Blything - £2351.12s.3d."

(signed). R.O. Brewster.

DARSHAM - 11 Nov 1642

Lent by:	Mrs Beddingfield in Plate	£20. 0. 0
	John Beddingfield in Plate	-
	William Hart Snr in Money & Plate	10. 0. 0
	William Haddenham in Money	10. 0. 0
	Walter Pilborough in Money	5. 0. 0
		£45. 0. 0
Given by:	John Eachard Cle. in Money & Plate	3. 2. 6
	Robert Browne in Money	1. 0. 0
	Robert Pooly in Money	1. 0. 0
	Divers other persons in Money & Plate	3. 4. 6
		£8. 7. 0

From DAVY's descriptions of Blything Hundred Vols 4 & 5

S.R.O.Ref: M/film J400/1

MUSTER ROLLS - 1638

Charles I

In 1637, Charles I had attempted to suppress Presbyterianism & Puritanism in Scotland and to impose uniformity of religion upon the nation. The Scots, determined to resist, collected an army and invaded England. To counter this uprising, lists of names were drawn up, of able men who were expected to arm themselves in times of trouble.

The list made in 1638, for the County of Suffolk, contains the names for:

DARSHAM

Jo: Bedingfeild Esq.
Roberte Browne
Robert Pooly
William Hadenham
- Jurden
James Britton
Jo: Shorte
Edw; Artis
Walter Pilborough
Thomas Stoklove
Henry Goodinge
William Chefton
Roberte Heyward
Jo: Bert
Dan: Allin
Valintine Perse
Ric: Mollett
Edm: Backleare
Ric: Botwrite
William Scoote
Nic: Benefild
Ric; Aldred
Peter Martin
Alex: Durrant
William Mosse

Thomas Bedingfield, gent
Thomas Steele
George Steele
William Tollifer
Ric: Dutt
Thomas Hart, gent.
Jo: Reeve, gent.
Henry Foster
Richard Cheston
Thomas Newston
Samuel Mowser
Jo: Brigges
Edw; Syers
An: Yorke
Gaudy Morris
William Wainford
Jo: Betch
Roberte Milles
Peter Aldrich
William Lord
Jo: Carter
George Mallet
Nic: Browne
William Burges
Edw: Pooley

WilliamHart,gent.
Jo: Baldery
Richard Baldery
George Crispe
Jo: Ellis
Philip Primrose
Arthur Ellis
William Reeve
Edward Mosse
Jo: Botwrite
Henry Canrum
Jo: Ellis, cons.

Transcribed from the original in the Public Record Office, London.
In the State Papers Domestic - Charles 1 vol.411.

Every parish elected its constable at the annual vestry meeting, and the constable was a key figure in keeping the King's peace. But the hard and fast rules of law and order had to be set against the equilibrium of the micro-society of the English village, and a balance had to be maintained.

In Act 3 Scene 3 of 'Much Ado About Nothing' Dogberry commends the Watch who plan to sleep through the night so that they do not disturb anybody. Dogberry adds: "you are to call at all the alehouses, and bid those that are drunk get them to bed." To which the Watch enquired: "How if they will not?" And the constable assures them: "Why then, let them alone till they are sober: if they make you not the better answer, you may say they are not the men you took them for." And when asked how to deal with a thief Dogberry advises : "The most peaceable way for you, if you do take a thief, is to let him show himself what he is, and steal out of your company." This non-interventionist approach allowed a community to be self-regulating instead of relying on a distant centralised authority.

A capacity for local independence can be illustrated by Vicar Eachard's pronouncement on the observance of Christmas. In 1644 Parliament tried to abolish Christmas — but John Eachard was adamant that Christmas should be observed enthusiastically, especially because of the miseries of the times. He wrote: "England shall keep that day of praising God, for the birth of Christ because the Angels sang an hymne on that day, 'Glory be to God on high, peace on earth, and good will towards men'; never more need for us, to pray and sing so; for peace is taken from the earth, and there is ill will towards men."

It would be attractive to think of Darsham as an island of harmony in this period, despite the turmoil and the miseries of England. But it is inevitable that many shadows of these times fell across the village. Particularly, the life of the village was played out against the threat of dearth. Periodic harvest disaster and food shortage haunted these times. It was not surprising that people were emigrating to the New World. Whatever difficulties they faced there, they were leaving behind an England of declining soil fertility, increasing population and recurrent anxieties with war in Europe and unrest in England. The weather was still a major factor. It alternated between severe flooding in winter and hot dry summers bringing drought. In 1606, lowland flooding resulted in 2,000 people drowned in the fens, followed by extreme frost everywhere. Rivers froze thick enough to bear horse and cart traffic, and in London fires were lit on the ice of the Thames when Frost Fairs were held.

Regular severe flooding followed by summer droughts, produced a scarcity of corn and hay; distress for farmers through low crop and land prices, and for the general population, food shortage and disease. In particular, during 1625 and again in 1636, plague was widespread.

There were so many factors that conspired to make the period 1600-1660 amongst the worst of times. An index has been constructed for real wages in England 1500-1912. This sequence takes account of commodity prices and the supply and demand of the labour market. The year 1507-8 is set at 1,000. The index then declines until the year 1593-4 to the 500's, but then plummets in the terrible years of 1596-7 as was mentioned in the last chapter, when the index sunk to 292. Thereafter, the index recovers for the years 1599 - 1647 so that it tends to hover in the upper 300's and lower 400's but then the sequence reads:

1647-8	366
1648-9	347
1649-50	342

After this it recovers into the 400's and 500's.
The index does not in fact recover again to the 1,000 mark until 1878-9, but still the dislocation of the years 1600 - 1660 can be understood in terms of the terrible social cost of unremitting hardship.

It is not surprising that in 1649 the King was executed — there was no grasp or understanding of economic life in those days. The King was accused of waging war on his people. Under the circumstances in which they were struggling, the people may well have felt under siege. Perhaps unconsciously, the King symbolised the repression that people felt so keenly. Yet his death was widely greeted with horror. Eventually the cult of 'King Charles the Martyr' developed, in which he was regarded as something like a sacrificial victim. The bad years never returned with such force and the Restoration of the Monarchy in 1660 ushered in a new era.

Chapter 6

The beginnings of Stability 1660 - 1760

One of the best ways of feeling 'in touch' with the past is to be able to know what people were talking about and to overhear their conversations. Apart from a few sermons of Vicar Eachard we cannot recover the words that were heard in Darsham in the seventeenth century. Whilst there is no record of concern over the imminent demise and extinction of the poor Dodo in far away Mauritius, far closer to home there would have been talk of hearing the naval guns at the Battle of Lowestoft on 3rd June 1665 during the 2nd Dutch War. Indeed, Samuel Pepys recorded in his diary that the noise of the guns could be heard in London. Then naval gunfire would have again been heard in Darsham at the Battle of Sole Bay, off Southwold, on 7th June 1672, during the 3rd Dutch War. Even earlier than this, and more importantly, was another matter and that was 'fire.'

In April, 1659, disaster had befallen the people of Southwold and much of their town was burnt down. Residents of Southwold were reduced to such poverty that in September 1660 the King gave permission for a national door-to-door collection in England and Wales to provide relief.

The Black Death of 1349 had been catastrophic. The plague of 1665 had nowhere near the same impact. Whilst the consequences were terrible in London and other various centres, this outbreak of plague may have carried fear rather than a sentence of death for residents of Darsham. One London Physician wrote that: "The whole British Nation wept for the Miseries of her Metropolis," [N. Hodges - Loimologia: or, an Historical Account of the Plague in London, 1665. Published 1720, p.16]. Fire was then back on the agenda in 1666 as news of the Great Fire of London came up the main road from London. That fire destroyed 13,200 homes and left about 80,000 people homeless.

Whilst Vicar Eachard's words are still available, maybe it is a good thing that some of the other words used in Darsham have not survived through the years of our history - particularly the actual words of one Mr John Snell, of Westleton. In 1682, he was charged with defamation before the Consistory Court of Norwich. It appears that Mr Snell had spread gossip that John Bishop and Catherine Aldus 'had unlawful carnal knowledge of each other's bodies' in a house in Blyford during the time that John Bishop was a lodger with Mr & Mrs Aldus. Nineteen witnesses gave evidence to the court saying, more or less, the same thing - that Mr Bishop a smythman, had formerly lodged at Cookley with Mr & Mrs Aldus and that after Mr Aldus died his widow, Mrs Catherine Aldus, married John Bishop, and that Mr Snell had said the words of which he was accused.

By the time that the case came before the Consistory Court, Mr and Mrs Bishop were living in Darsham so Mr Snell was sentenced to do penance in the parish church of Darsham after divine service one Sunday. In the presence of the Churchwardens, repeating after the minister, he had to say: "I John Snell do humbly confess to Almighty God and before these persons present that being transported with passion I did contrary to the rules of Charity and good manners utter certain diffamatory words tending to the Diffamation of Mrs Catherine Bishop the wife of Mr John Bishop and of her good name and reputation for the speaking of which words I am heartily sorry and pray Almighty God to give me grace never to commit the like offence again." [TNA Ref: DEL 1/170 Snell v Bishop - Court Report]

However, the socio-economic history of Darsham is more than local gossip. The challenge is to fit surviving information into a regional context. The first thing to grasp is the small scale on which Darsham was operating. This can be illustrated by the local coinage. In the years around the start of the period covered by this chapter there was a national shortage of small coins. The result was that local tradesmen issued 'Trade Tokens' to make up the deficiency. These tokens were a mixture of halfpence and farthings and were important not just for what they could buy but because they rescued the local economy from relying on the system of barter. In the immediate locality, tokens were issued at Dunwich, Yoxford, Sibton, Halesworth and Saxmundham. It was not until 1672 that good national coinage drove these local tokens out of use.

Even though local poverty was still rife, Darsham folk still tried to be generous. In 1674 a collection was made in Darsham church which amounted to the sum of £10. 7s. 9d for the relief of the poor of Halesworth when visited by the Smallpox. The Hearth Tax list for that same year showed that in Darsham, 34 people paid the tax of 2 shillings half yearly, and that 27 poor households were exempt, suggesting that there might be 55 to 60 households. It was recorded in 1708/09 that there were 104 people over the age of 16 years of age in the parish — 47 men and 57 women. During the preceding 16 years the baptisms of 75 children were recorded, suggesting a total population of 179, but by 1717, perhaps more accurately, the Vicar's Annual Report records that the population then numbered 236.

Perhaps the strongest impressions from the start of this period in 1660 is the small-scale nature of much of East Anglian farming and the gradual change over the years. One simple statistic underlines this consideration. One researcher found that less than one per cent of farmers in Norfolk and Suffolk possessed a waggon in the 1660's, but by the 1720's nearly 30 per cent of farmers had a

DARSHAM HEARTH TAX - 1674

A tax of 2/- p.a., payable half-yearly, was levied on each hearth in the occupation of people who were ratepayers of church and poor rates, whose house was worth more than 20/- p.a . The poor were exempt from paying, but they had to obtain a certificate of exemption from the local clergyman, churchwardens and overseers, signed by 2 JPs.

NAME	NO OF HEARTHS			
The Lady Beddingfield	18			
Jo. Carter	5			
Mr Aldred	4			
Richard Mullett	3			
James Canham	2			
Widow Pooley	2			
Robert Salthorne	2			
Widow Odby	2			
Sim Crispe	2			
Thomas Howe	4			
Thomas Hammond	2			
William Micklebrowne	4			
Sam Gotes	2			
Widow Browne	4	Exemptions		
Edward Pooley	7	(Certificate of Poverty)		
Mat. Burwood	4			
Nich. Browne	4	Nich.Woods	2 }	
Thomas Hurren	2	Thos.Goodwin	2 }	4
Henry Beale	1			
Widow Browne	3	Ro.Cookwith	2 }	
Thomas Abbey	2	Widow Wight	2 }	4
Edmund Watlinge	2			
Henry Short	2	Sa.Mouncer	1 }	
Mr Woodward	6	Nich. Brewse	2 }	3
Richard Mallett	2			
Jo. Lambe	2	Widow Harper	1 }	
Richard Pecke	3	Thomas Pettit	2 }	3
Arthur Ellis}				
Ph. Primrose}	2	Eliz Lambe		2
Edward Mansell	2			
Richard Crispe	2	That receive collection		11
Robert Plawe	2	(Parish Relief)		
Nich. Bruster	2			
Sam Mosse	2			
	---------			----------
	108			27

JOHN SNELL, gent. of Westleton sentenced by the Consistory Court to perform his Penitence in Darsham Church - on 1st Aug. 1682

"A schedule of Pennance to be performed by John Snell of Westleton, gent, as followeth."

> 'The said Mr John Snell shall upon some Sunday before the next Consistorie Courte at Norwich imediately after Divine Service and Sermon in the parish Church of Darsham before the Minister and Churchwardens there. Mrs Bishop first having notice of the same make this Confession as followeth. the Minister in his Reading Desk and the said Mr Snell in the Alley saying after him. I John Snell do humbly confess to Almighty God and before these persons present that being transported with passion I did contrary to the rules of Charity and good manners utter certain deffamatory words tending to the Deffamation of Mrs Catherine Bishop the wife of Mr John Bishop and of her good name and reputation for the speaking of which words I am heartily sorry and pray Almighty God to give me grace never to commit the like offence again. The performance hereof is to be certifyed at or before the next Consistory Court at Norwich being the 26th Day of September 1682 under the hands of the persons that were present att the performance thereof.'

PRO Ref: DEL 1/170 Snell v Byshop - Defamation cause 1683 - the Court report.

waggon. This meant that in 1660, most farm produce in Darsham would have been moved by small two-wheeled carts and tumbrils and sledges rather than by the more grand four-wheeled wagons. We have to forget Constable's Haywain picture and instead see a mosaic of small fields and open land worked communally feeding the local population with small surpluses for sale or barter. It was not until the death of Michael Willson in Darsham in 1721, when we have the mention of a waggon in the inventory of his effects, that there is any evidence that Darsham's agriculture had developed sufficiently for there to be any local need of a waggon.

One development that may have increased production on Darsham's heavier soils was the introduction of 'under-draining'. By this practice, parallel trenches were cut across fields on the line of the slope. Branches or loose stones were laid at the bottom of the trenches which were then filled up with earth. These 'under drains' discharged into deep open ditches. It is almost certain that surviving deep ditches in Darsham owe their origin to under-draining. It was recorded that under-draining was well established in Suffolk in 1769, and could have figured in Darsham some years before this date.

Another factor of which one has to take into account was the weather — scarcely surprising in a farming community! In the later 1600's, we suffered a 'Little Ice Age', with the most extreme conditions of winter cold and summer wetness in the 1690's. This presented farmers with a dilemma — how to produce adequate fodder for animals. If the weather wrecked the harvest, they needed something to cover for when beasts could not be grazed. The solution was the humble turnip. If the hay harvest proved disappointing, turnips could be sown in August to provide fodder in the winter months.

From the mid-1500's to 1750, it was required by law that the Probate Court be provided with an inventory of a deceased persons moveable goods which included his crops and animals and some of these inventories have survived for Darsham farmers. So it was that if turnips had been grown, they would only figure in inventories made during the winter time. Turnips first appear for Darsham in the inventory of the possessions of the late John Smith in December 1714, again in February 1742 (for the late Thomas Aldrid), and in November 1729 (for the late John Mollett of Darsham Hall Farm & Trustan's Farm). Turnips had moved from the kitchen garden to being a field crop.

It is worth reproducing the comments of Daniel Defoe that he recorded in 1722 on a visit to this area: "This part of England is also remarkable for being the first where the feeding and fattening of cattle, both sheep as well as black cattle, with turnips, was first practised in England, which is made a very great part of the improvement of their lands to this day, and from whence the practice is

from part of the Inventory of John Mollett buried at Darsham 13 Nov 1729

SRO Ref: FE1 /21 / 28

At Gravel-pit Farm

Item	For Three Haystacks	£21. 0.0
Item	For Turnips upon the ground	21. 5.0
Iten	For nine Acres of Rye upon the Common	4. 0.0
Item	For Two Cows & two Steers at Turnips	12.15.0
Item	For a Boarded Cott a Tumbrell & 2 Harrows	6. 7.0
Item	For a Bushell & two Fans	10.0
Item	For an Iron Skuppet two Dudfins	10.0
Item	For Two Rowls	10.0

Corn in Barns & Stacks amounted as followeth.

	Ten Score & four Comb of Barly	£71.14.0
Item	Eleven Comb of Oats	4. 8.0
Item	Nine Comb & an half of Pease 15(s)p C	7. 2.6
Item	Twenty two Comb of Wheat at 13(s)p C	14. 6.0
Item	Half a Load of Cheese & Butter	8. 0.6

Gravel-pit Farm.

Item For three Haystacks — 21·0·0
Item For Turnips upon the Grounde — 21·5·0
Item For nine Acres of Rye upon ye Common — 4·0·0
Item For two Cows & two Steers at Turnips — 12·15·0
Item For a Boarded Cott a Tumbrell & 2 Harrows &c — 6·7·0
Item For a Bushell & two Fans — 0·10·0
Item For an Iron Skuppet two Dudfins &c — 0·10·0
Item For two Rowls — 0·10·0

Corn in Barns & Stacks amounted as followeth. Ten Score & four Comb of Barly — 71·14·0
Item — Eleven Comb of Oats — 4·8·0
Item — Nine Comb & an half of Pease 15s p C — 7·2·6
Item — Twenty two Comb of Wheat at 13s p C — 14·6·0
Item — Half a Load of Cheese & Butter — 8·0·6

334:01:6
88:9:8
Totall 422:11:2

whose names are Underwritten

The mark of John X [illegible]
John Row

Annual Rents for Farms on the Estate of Darsham cum Yoxford at 21st October, 1706

	£
Dame Mary Knyvett for Darsham Hall & Lands	120. 00
Farms:	
Robert Ralls	50. 00
Bryant Copland	40 00
John Smyth	40. 00
John Aldrich	40. 00
Peter Specks	10. 00
Thomas Winter	16. 00
Elizabeth Pettitt (Widow)	12. 00
Robert Pettitt	6. 00
John Canham	5. 10s
Margaret Skeets	15. 00
Elizabeth Veale (Widow)	6. 16s
Thomas Mills	5. 00
John Mollitt	43. 00
Elizabeth Hammont (Widow)	1. 10s

S.R.O. Ref: HB 26/ 412 / 322

spread over the east and south parts of England to the great enriching of the farmers and increase of fat cattle. And though some have objected against the goodness of the flesh thus fed with turnips, and have fancied it would taste of the root, yet upon experience it is found that at market there is no difference, nor can they that buy single out one joint of mutton from another by the taste." [Daniel Defoe, Tour Through the Eastern Counties of England, Cassell 1888 pp,120,121].

Defoe mentioned: "Halesworth, Saxmundham, Debenham, Aye or Eye, all standing in this eastern side of Suffolk, in which ..... the whole country is employed in dairies or in feeding of cattle." [ibid.p.120]

Interestingly, there is no record of clover being grown in Darsham in this period. Clover was the other major crop introduced into Norfolk and Suffolk in this era. So Darsham did not yet see the so-called 'Norfolk four-course rotation' of wheat, turnips, barley and clover.

Given the small scale of Darsham farming, it is unlikely that anything was produced for the London market until into the 1700's. Most inventories listed a sprinkling of animals, normally a few cows and horses and a 'hogg.' But things changed for the 1720's. An inventory of 1721 recorded one farmer (the late Michael Willson) with 20 cows and 14 heifers, and another of 1729 (the late John Mollett again) with 2 heiffers and 23 milch cows, and another of 1734 (the late Francis Martin of Home Farm) with 8 milch cows and 2 heiffers. These animals may well have helped to supply the trade in butter and cheese for the London market.

The negative effects of enclosure do not appear to have been felt in Darsham, perhaps because here it was a gradual process, and by the eighteenth century it may already have been almost completed. However the increase in dairy farming may well be one of its positive effects. Enclosure would have meant that cows and bulls could be separated. In this way breeding programmes could be initiated which would produce animals capable of higher milk production. Lactation periods could be regularised ensuing more continuous milk production. Pasture could be improved by a system of manuring, and rotation of crops could be introduced. All this lead to considerably increased yields, consequently there was the opportunity for trade with London.

Eighteenth century writers calculated that in 1730 Londoners consumed 56,703 firkins of Suffolk butter and 985 tons of Suffolk cheese. It is to be hoped that Darsham had its fair share of income from the appetite of the mushrooming population of London. Perhaps we may wonder how Darsham produce could have travelled to London — well, Defoe recorded the answer in 1722: " .... Dunwich, however ruined, retains some share of trade, as particularly for the shipping of butter, cheese and corn, which is so great a business in this county for butter .... All the counties of England contribute something towards the subsistence of .... London, of which butter here is a very considerable article; as also is cheese ...., used chiefly for the King's ships." [ibid p.113]

Another regional effect of the London market was the practice of fattening cattle from far away counties. Scottish beasts were particularly important. The drovers brought the cattle down from Scotland, over the Pennines and down to east Anglia where they rented thousands of acres of pasture for grazing. Whether or not they grazed the fields of Darsham, or whether they were taken through the village by drovers and could merely be nourished from the wayside cannot be known, but this trade became important as London grew and grew. " In terms of sheer numbers the population of the metropolis increased from about 200,000 in 1600 to perhaps 350,000 - 400,000 in 1650 and 575,000 - 600,000 in 1700. By the beginning of the 18th century London contained ten per cent of the national population, and up to 650,000 in 1750." [The London Encyclopaedia 1983. p.613]

But by the mid 1700's the trade of droving was taken up by the some of the local butchering families, for example, Robert Higham of Bramfield, Alexander Milbourne of Southwold, Henry Nursey of Halesworth, and the Churchyard family of Melton, who advertised their trade of salesmen and drovers, taking local cattle to Smithfield. Their route through Suffolk started at Wangford, collecting stock at The White Hart, Blythburgh, The Griffin, Yoxford, on Tuesdays; the Horse and Groom, Benhall, The Chaise & Pair, Wickham Market, the Crown at Ufford on Wednesdays and at Ipswich on Thursdays. Advertisements were taken in the Ipswich Journal encouraging local farmers to sell their cattle to the local butchers who were commissioned by the Smithfield salesmen for the best prices.

Chapter 7

Darsham fell off the map! 1761 - 1837

In 1760 George III succeeded to the throne. In 1757, the first edition of a new travel book had been published. It took an established series of English maps by John Ogilby and turned them into a pocket book, in which were "delineated all the cities, towns, villages, hills, rivers, brooks, churches, capital seats and every place worthy of note throughout each road."

This new work by John Senex, went through several editions. It shows clearly the road from London to Yarmouth leaving Yoxford, going past Darsham Church, through 'Brussl Green,' 'Hinton Street Common,' and then intersecting with roads to Dunwich and 'Hestbridg.' No-one in those days was expected to take a detour to Westleton!

It is easy to visualise a new breed of traveller, pocket book in hand, riding through Darsham on the way to Blythburgh and Yarmouth. However about fifty years later in 1811, a new map was published by Daniel Paterson. This shows the new turnpike road, which had by then been open for twenty-six years. It leaves Yoxford and the next place mentioned is .... Wrentham! Darsham had fallen off the map.

Even so this chapter must recount what happened in Darsham between 1761 and 1837 whilst the rest of the world hurried by. Perhaps it gives a clue as to what is to come to realise that we have also to take account of what was going on up the road at the 'House of Industry' — the workhouse at Bulcamp.

However, we started by mentioning roads. The roads of England were ancient, and inadequate for a developing economy. The highway was a mere right of passage for every subject of the Crown over another's land. It was not, as is the case in the present day, a clearly defined strip of land designated as a road. Passage and re-passage was a communal property right. Maintenance was a parochial responsibility and stone-picking for mending the roads was the occupation of women and children. From 1555 each parish was required to meet annually and elect two unpaid "Surveyors of the Highways" who had to supervise and direct the teams of labour who were meant to report for duty as required by law. Darsham would be responsible for maintaining the roads within its boundaries — but there was commonly not much willingness to maintain roads that were for the benefit of people passing through a parish. Local people would have felt that there was little return to be had for maintaining the London to Yarmouth road when only rare occasions might have taken them as far as Yoxford.

Other factors affecting this system of maintenance may

have been the lack of training and lack of expertise in civil engineering. Some 'repairs' actually made the road worse! This was indeed the case years later in 1877. At the Yoxford Petty Sessions, two Darsham highway surveyors, Frederick Hayward, tenant farmer at Darsham Hall, and William Robinson, the miller, were charged with neglect of repairing the road leading from Yoxford towards Darsham. It was suggested that "......they had actually picked up the sides of the road to repair the centre." It transpired that the boundary between the parishes was down the centre of the road and that a verbal agreement had been made that Darsham would keep the road in good repair. Although this was later denied, the magistrates said that even a verbal agreement was morally binding, and that the whole of the highway between the parishes should be divided instead by a traverse line, and ordered 'each parish to repair the roadway thereof.' The magistrates told the parties that if the matter was not settled amicably, further proceedings would be taken.

By the end of the eighteenth century, a national network of turnpike roads was gradually spreading across the country. A turnpike road was organised by appointed trustees who were allowed to borrow the necessary capital for the project and set tolls to repay their borrowing and to pay their staff and maintenance. Each turnpike required an Act of Parliament. The development of the A.12 between Ipswich & Yarmouth began in 1784. In the early part of that year a group of local landowners in the north of the county had formed themselves into a committee, lead by Sir John Rous of Henham & Darsham, to promote the establishment of a Turnpike from Ipswich to Southtown. They planned to build toll-gates and toll-houses along the road. Initially, the suggestion was that the turnpike should pass through the parishes from Ipswich, via Woodbridge, Melton, Wickham Market, Saxmundham Yoxford, Darsham and Blythburgh, thence via Bulcamp to Beccles, into Norfolk via Haddiscoe, and back into Suffolk via Bradwell to Southtown. There was a worry that the cost would fall heavily upon those parishes without their receiving any benefit. It was therefore decided by several local landowners to form another committee under the chairmanship of Richard Frank, to oppose the plan totally because the proposed turnpike would add a further burden and unnecessary extra tax. It was proposed that Mr John Revett of Brandeston Hall confer with those in favour of the turnpike. However those in favour won and the Turnpike opened in 1785.

The trustees appointed to organise the new turnpike included Sir John Rous of Henham and Darsham Hall, and Eleazer Davy of Yoxford. The trust employed a clerk at £40 per year, a surveyor at a guinea per day for not more than 50 days per year, and a foreman. Darsham had two tollgates, both were at the 'Stone Cottages' at the modern junction of the A.12 and the A.144, one collecting tolls on

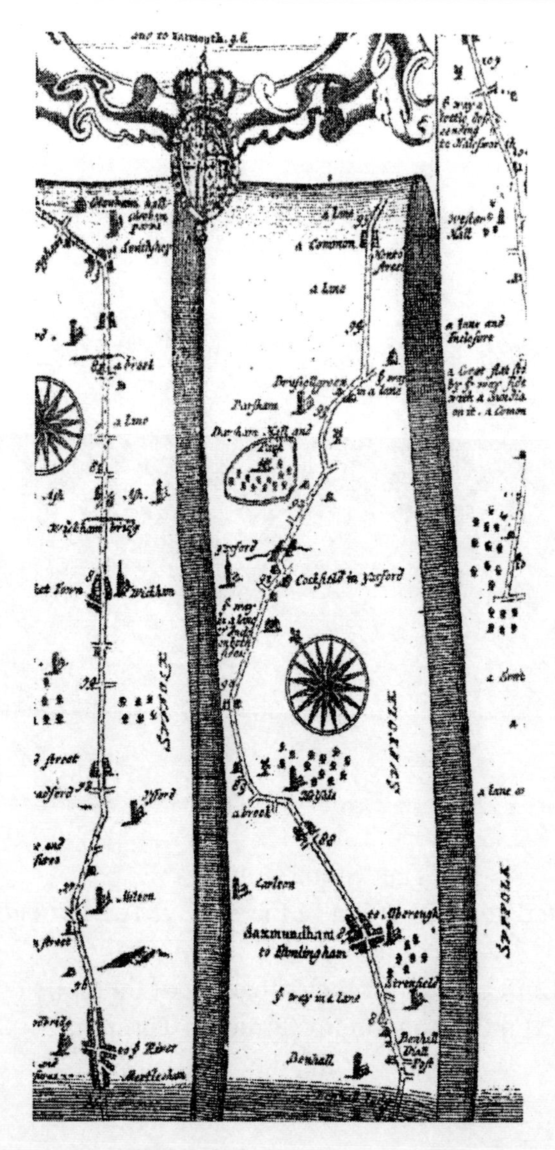

Part of John Ogilby's Strip Map c.1675 showing the London to Yarmouth Road passing through Darsham

S.R.O. Ref: HB 26/ 412 / 322

The ‘Stone Cottages’
Situated at the junction of the A.12 & A.143 roads.

Built c.1785 for the collection of the Tolls
on the London to Yarmouth Turnpike
and the
Beech Lane to Bungay Turnpike

the road to and from Yarmouth, and another for the branch turnpike to Bungay.

The authority of turnpike trusts was of limited duration and their powers had to be renewed by Parliament. 'Our' original Act of Parliament (25 Geo 3 cap.116) was continued (47 Geo 3 sess.2.cap.49) and renewed (9 Geo 4 cap.45).

Though the trustees achieved their general aim in opening the new turnpike, it did not follow their favoured route. At Beccles a large majority of the population and local landowners had been against the turnpike coming within 8 miles of the town. Robert Sparrow was totally against the project. John Farr, landowner at Beccles, was in favour of the road stopping short of the town and wanted it diverted at Bulcamp. Miles Barne of Sotterley Hall, Sir John Rous and Bence Sparrow wanted the road to come through the town. The Beccles objectors obviously won their case to the extent that the road was routed as it is today diverting at Bulcamp via Wangford, Wrentham & Lowestoft.

Where a new highway was established, old highways could disappear back into fields across which they had passed. Thus the route from Brussels Green to Hinton has been lost and Brussels Green has been become a quiet lane leading only to Green Farm. Darsham people were relieved from maintaining a road that they might never have used but which they were doomed to repair.

'Our' turnpikes were known as the 'Ipswich to Southtown' and the 'Darsham to Bungay'. Both were serviceable but were never intended to create a profit. For example, in 1834 the total income was £2,694 whilst the total expenditure was £2,872. However the turnpikes did succeed in providing an improved passage for travellers and goods and this benefited the parishes through which the turnpike passed, as well as others nearby. The stagecoaches and the Royal Mail were able to run a more regular service.

It is remarkable how well Darsham was provided with connections to London. In 1800, a publication called 'Holden's Annual List,' recording the coaches, waggons, carts, etc., that radiated out from London, showed two weekly waggons and two daily coaches that stopped at Darsham. Yoxford, in this list, had 5 daily coaches, 5 weekly waggons and two mail coaches each day. Westleton, alas, was not listed but would, no doubt, have sent a waggon to meet the coaches and the mail. By the 1830s, a well developed network of stage coaches meant that Yarmouth to the Three Tuns Inn at Yoxford took 3¾ hours; Yoxford to Aldgate in London took 11¾ hours, including stops for meals and a change of horses.

However whilst progress in creating better travelling conditions and a new road network are interesting, our

TURNPIKE (A.12 road) OPENED 1785
IPSWICH to SOUTHTOWN
& GREAT YARMOUTH
also
BEECH LANE FARM, DARSHAM, to BUNGAY

The Trustees include:

Sir John Rous, bart., - Later became the 1st Earl of Stradbroke.
Sir Gerrard Vaneck, bart., - father of the 1st Baronet Huntingfield.
Eleazer Davy Esq., of The Grove, Yoxford - Antiquary whose collection of papers on Suffolk are in the British Museum.

The Trust employed:

Clerk at £40 per year.
Surveyor at £1. 1. 0d per day on not more than 50 days per year.
Foreman over a gang of 60 men at £1. 10. 0d per week.
Foreman over a gang of 20 men at 12/- per week.

TOLLHOUSES

A Tollhouse at the West side of the road at Saxmundham
- built by Isaac Ablett, carpenter & John Booth, bricklayer
- both of Saxmundham.

'View Cottage' at the Northern end of Blythburgh Dam - at the junction of A.12 & A.143. Rented as a Tollhouse from Sir John Rous. Demolished in 1966.

'Flint Cottages' at the junction of the A.12 & A.144.

TURNPIKE TARIFF

1. Every Horse, Gelding, Mare, Mule or other beast, drawing any Coach Chariot, Landau, Berlin, Hearse, Chaise, Calash or any suchlike carriage. Being charged Excise Duty.. 3 pence

2. Every Horse, Gelding, Mare ... as above. Laden or Unladen not drawing any Coach, Chariot ... as above.. 1 penny

3. For every drove of Oxen, Cows etc... .....10 pence per score

4. For every drove of Calves, Sheep, Lambs, Hogs or Swine..5 pence per score

5. His Majesty & Royal Family .... No Toll

6. Materials for road building .... No Toll

7. No Toll on Manure, except Lime; None on Agricultural produce not for sale; None on Horses employed in Husbandry; None on Funerals; Those escorting vagrants to the Workhouse; or prisoners to Gaol.

The HIGHWAYS ACT of 1555 transferred the upkeep of the King's highways to the parish who appointed a Surveyor, usually a reluctant farmer, and every able bodied parishioner was obliged to give 4 days (increased to later to 6 days) unpaid labour each year, to the repair of the roadways. However it was possible to pay a fine in lieu or to provide a paid substitute. The HIGHWAYS ACT of 1835 abolished this statutory labour and levied a Highway Rate.

concern must be to report as much as we can of the lot of local people for whom such developments had relatively little significance. The records of the national price of wheat are useful in this respect. The price of wheat is a key indicator of the price of food, and during this period the cost of wheat varied in ways that would have been catastrophic for anyone on a low income. Malnutrition would have been the least of the possible outcomes. During the first thirty years of George III's reign until the beginning of the war with France the price of wheat varied with the weather. This would produce price fluctuations of up to one third from year to year. The price ranged from 30 shillings and 54 shillings for a quarter of wheat. In the years from 1795 until the Battle of Waterloo in 1815, the price of wheat rose as high as 184 shillings per quarter. By 1836 the range of wheat prices had dropped back to between 39 shillings and 69 shillings. Such figures conceal a mountain of misery from which people of Darsham were not exempt.

A 'quarter' was 28 pounds weight. Since 1266, legislation for 'the Assize of Bread and Ale' had regulated the weight of the Farthing Loaf, and the quantity of a Penny of Ale according to the price of the ingredients. Bakers and Brewers who gave short measure could be fined, put in the pillory or flogged. When the price of wheat reached 100 shillings per quarter, a farthing would buy less than one tenth of an ounce of flour, and the small loaf weighing one pound would cost more than 3s 6d. The comparison of this figure with the wages recorded for these times stirs up an appalling vision of mass deprivation.

> '41 weeks of winter at 6s 5d per week; six weeks of 'haytime' at 9s 5d per week, and for the five weeks of harvest at 10s 8d per week. The equivalent figures for women labourers were 3s, 4s. 4d, and 6s. 3d respectively. Farm servants, living-in and paid by the year were found to average £10 8s 6d for 'first' men; £6 11s 0d for 'second' men; £3 2s 0d for lads; £3 19s 0d for dairymaids; and £3 5s 0d for other female servants on a farm.'

These figures worked out in 1770 by a man called Arthur Young overlap with the information provided by the Henham Hall account books for 1777-1794 of Sir John Rous who employed various local people. Annually, a butler could be paid £42; a footman 15 guineas; a coachman 21 guineas; a groom 17 guineas; a stable boy 9 guineas; a gardener £20. The boy who worked in the kitchen was paid about the same as the lad who worked on a farm - 3 guineas a year, but the 'indoor' female servants, like the men, were paid much better than their farming equivalents. A 'helper and dairymaid' received £9 per year; the cook £10 per year; the housekeeper £20 per year. Those employees who 'lived-in' would have had their food provided and all would have had a uniform supplied. When Arthur Young visited Suffolk in 1794, he found that day labourers were being paid 1s 4d per day in winter, 1s

6d per day in summer and 2s 10d in harvest. A different pattern was emerging with people only being paid when there was work, hence the figures for day labour. The old practice whereby single labourers boarded at the farmhouse was being snuffed out by the high price of food in wartime. The appalling prices of 1800/1801, and the food shortages meant that many farmers ceased to feed their men when it was hardest for them to feed themselves.

In an island at war there was great pressure on farmers to maximise production. There was also the incentive of high prices. Local farmers did their best to respond and experimented by varying agricultural practices. A record is preserved of three Darsham farmers in 1803 trying to get the best out of their fields and of their use of seed drills. (Arthur Young - General View of the Agriculture of the County of Suffolk 1804 pp 403 - 405). The underlying implication derived from this record is of an attempt to control production costs by minimising the use of labour.

In a changing world, Messrs Read, Martin & Gooch tried to balance the need to feed humans, horses and bullocks. Searching for a balance between levels of production and production methods, they even managed to avoid ploughing before every crop in a rotation. Mr Martin's basic rotation was recorded as:

Turnips (dunged), Barley, Clover or Beans, and Wheat (dunged).

As well as the pressure on the price of food, wages and technical innovation, the war generated huge social pressures. There was a climate of suspicion. In 1793, local magistrates ordered the Publicans of Blything Hundred to report on any seditious clubs and societies. Meanwhile wages never kept pace with prices. Then, on the 26th June 1801, the Times newspaper of London reported the suicide of Mr Danbrook, 'a respectable shopkeeper of Yoxford' who shot himself at his breakfast table in the presence of his wife and the local surgeon. On the 8th November, 1802, the Times noted a dividend being paid to the creditors of Mr Cunningham, a grocer of Yoxford. Bankruptcy and suicide up the road indicated a local economy in deep trouble.

Trading conditions were so bad that Mr Gooch, the farmer, and another farmer Thomas Kent of Darsham Hall, both had to sell up in 1805. In 1807, even John Cross, the miller of Darsham, went under. Even so, Darsham had a generous heart, and despite sustained hardship in 1811 the parish sent £4. 15s 6d for the relief of British prisoners in France.

Parliamentary records enable us to chart the impact of overwhelming poverty on local society. In 1764, when the Blything Union was formed, it was calculated that the average annual expenditure for Darsham on our poor was £54 13s 4d. The average total for all of the Blything parishes came to £3,084 12s 11d. A workhouse was built at Bulcamp near Blythburgh in the hope that it would be a more cost-effective way of catering for the needs of the poor. Apart from the year 1795/96, this level of expenditure continued until 1799/1800. Then the expenditure in the union usually fell within the range of five to eight thousand pounds until 1815/16 when expenditure shot up to around £13,000. It did not fall below £10,000 again until 1826/27, and only remained at these lower levels for three years before climbing back up again. These cost were a colossal burden on the local economy.

In 1816, the Board of Agriculture published 'The Agricultural State of the Kingdom', and included the following comment by Thomas Taylor of Westwood, Yoxford:

> "The heavy arrears of rent which the tenants are obliged to leave with their landlord; their not being able to pay their tradesmen's bills; and the great number of labourers which are thrown out of employ; added to this the great number of assignments made every week by farmers of their stock, etc. for the benefit of their creditors; with a variety of circumstances, prove the distress of the farmer to be so great, that they may be considered, generally, as insolvent.

> Dairy farmers up to last Michaelmas, did not suffer much, because the price of cheese and butter was high up to that period; but since Michaelmas the price of butter has declined 40 per cent, and the dairy farmers begin to complain loudly.
>
> From the inability of both farmers and tradesmen to employ the labouring poor, vast numbers by orders from magistrates, are working on the roads, but from the inadequacy of the pay allowed them to support their families (though this is with the utmost difficulty found by the parishes) they have lately assembled in considerable bodies, demanding with an urgency which indicates approaching riot and tumult, further relief."

The impact of poverty was intensified by the poor relief process through which those who still had money had to pay for the increasing number that had nothing. This was a process of ruination. For the years 1810-1815, the annual cost for Darsham for 'out-relief' ranged from £64 to £84, but from 1815-1818 this cost shot up to range between £175 and £195. Up until 1832, this charge to the parish never dropped below £100. 'Out-relief' was paid to those who were not 'in' the workhouse. In 1820, the Poor Relief Book for Darsham records that Thomas Burgess was allowed 18 shillings for his wife's funeral; William Yallop, was allowed 7 shillings to bury his two-year-old child; and in 1821, two unemployed men were each allowed 8 shillings for four weeks when their wives were in childbed.

In 1831, Darsham was credited with a population of 513. In 1830, 305 of the residents were categorised as paupers. Basically, that meant that 60% of our inhabitants were so poor that the life of Darsham was dominated by poverty. The Blything Hundred had a population of 24,177 in 1831 and in 1830, 11,891 of them were listed as paupers. On the basis of the percentage numbers of paupers in a parish, Darsham was just about the poorest place in the whole Hundred. Darsham was being ruined and poverty was systemic. Living on relief had become a way of life passed down through the generations. The Second Annual Report of the Poor Law Commissioners' of 1836 included the following paragraph about a Darsham widow:—

> "Mary White was admitted to the poorhouse at Bulcamp, 28th September, 1795, a widow, (and still is an inmate of the house); she had three children with her, Elizabeth, Susan and James, belonging to Darsham; James died 13th April 1807; Elizabeth married, and she and her family belonged to Blythburgh; Susan, after her marriage (with her family) belonged to Theberton, who still remained in the house. The time the widow, her children and her children's children have been inmates of this house, amounts to 11,102 weeks, 5 days, up to June 1836."

Against a background of poverty and food scarcity reports are preserved of food riots, machine breaking, and rick burning, and so on. Rioters were hanged at Ely and Bury-St-Edmunds in 1816. Deep discontent surfaced in isolated protest and low-level crime as people crossed the threshold where they could not face any more suffering. Locally, the crunch year seemed to have been 1822. Landowners had to help to calm the countryside by giving undertakings not to use machines for a year. Threshing machines were hated particularly, because the old methods of threshing by hand on the winnowing floor needed a large local labour force, and women and children could be employed. It was often the only work that there was in winter. Landowners in Yoxford and Blythburgh had to undertake not to use these machines. A report in the Times of December 30th, 1822, might have been typical of these troubles. 20 combs of wheat had been stolen at Sibton. A few days later the owner received back the empty sacks with a note containing the lines:—

"We have got your wheat,
And you can't find it:
'Twas a famous wind,
That helped to grind it."

Ill-feeling continued to simmer locally, fanning the flames of personal grudges and petty disputes. Neighbouring Westleton was perhaps even more irrepressible than Darsham, and it is recorded that Benjamin Edwards and James Strowger were hanged at Ipswich in August 1832 for 'setting fire to an out-house, stable, barn, and other buildings, in the occupation of Mr Adolphus Stanford, at Westleton, Suffolk, on the night of the 30th April last'.

As a general principle, education was seen in these times as a remedy both for unrest and poverty. In 1821 there were the early stirrings of what became the 'self-help' movement when William Cobbett wrote his 'Cottage Economy'. This splendid guide, dedicated to enabling the poor to improve their situation, covered a wonderful range of topics with simple, clear instructions. The fact that the book opened with the subject of brewing beer and then of making bread should have given it a wide appeal. It might seem strange that Cobbett had to remind cottagers how to make bread, but he had found that people were using potatoes as a cheap alternative perhaps because for the previous twenty years the price of wheat had been beyond their means. However, this book itself could not address a more basic problem — people had to be able to read so as to receive the benefit of this book.

In 1816, parliamentary returns from the parish clergy show that in Darsham there was a Sunday School for 30 children, supported by voluntary contributions. In 1833, the first Educational Grant Bill was passed to set up National Schools for elementary education, but it is not clear when the benefits of this legislation had arrived in Darsham. However, by 1835 things had changed. Now Darsham had one daily school containing 25 boys and girls, instructed "at the expense of their parents." This automatically excluded the totally poor and compounded their disadvantage. In 1846, we find that Miss Elizabeth Snell was the teacher, but where they assembled is unclear, perhaps in the church, for Darsham was not to have a purpose-built school until 1854.

Education was going to be one of the great challenges of the nineteenth century — particularly the problem of securing real standards. Teachers had to be trained and become qualified. Amazingly, by 1850 there were only 1,173 certified teachers in the whole of England, Wales and Scotland. We had a long way to go. However, let this chapter end with some good news: A report in the Bury Herald was picked up for inclusion in the Times of 3rd April, 1837 — Bulcamp Workhouse was abolishing the treadmill! Something was getting better!

Chapter 8

Darsham back on the map! 1837 - 1914

The writing of books about Victorian times and the Edwardian age has become quite an industry. It is all very well for us to chorus 'Land of Hope and Glory' - but most of our ancestors were tied to the soil, and life was hard. We have to commend such books as Pamela Horn's "Labouring Life in the Victorian Countryside" (1976) for offering an all-round look at rural life in those days. However, the purpose of this chapter is to complement the huge literature available with some insight into life in and around Darsham.

Darsham was part of the Deanery of Dunwich, part of the registration district of Westleton, and part of the Blything Hundred. In 1850, the Hundred was made up of 45 parishes, ranging from Covehithe in the north to Leiston in the south and Huntingfield in the west, including Halesworth and Kelsale but excluding Saxmundham. The Hundred contained about 91,500 acres with a population of around 26,000.

The East Suffolk Constabulary had been established in 1840 with its headquarters at Yoxford, and the Chief Constable had 63 men under his command, all constables who were locally appointed. Petty Sessions courts were held at Yoxford and Halesworth. Lest it be thought that the parishioners of Darsham were always well behaved, records show that it had its share of miscreants.

The pursuit of game was a constant problem, transportation to the colonies had been discontinued by 1850 and fines were substituted. A fine of £1 with 8s 6d costs was almost two week's wages and if not paid immediately, then the sentence could be 2 months imprisonment with hard labour. However, although poaching was done by some as 'one for the pot,' a few poachers appear to have treated it as a way to challenge authority, and as a result the same names regularly came up to court. Drunk and disorderly on the Highway was another regular offence, particularly if in charge of a horse. Failure to send a child to school received a fine of 6d with 4s 6d costs, but with time given to pay.

In 1867, 13 year old Martha Newson of Darsham was found guilty of stealing a chemise and other articles valued at 2s 6d. She was imprisoned at Ipswich Gaol and kept to hard labour for two months. Two cases of chicken stealing brought sentences of imprisonment with hard labour. Stealing was looked upon very seriously and almost always resulted in imprisonment with hard labour.

Wilful damage and assault over neighbours quarrels were regular occurrences. In 1893 a disturbance occurred in the Street between Mr Mountain, the Postmaster & Builder, and his neighbour Mr Noller, the carpenter. It transpired that Mrs Mountain had put some carpet out to dry on the dividing hedge. Mr Noller claimed that this had damaged the hedge and abusive language was used by both sides, whereupon Mr Mountain's daughter threw water over Mr Noller. Both sides appeared in court, each suing the other over the use of the hedge, both sides were found guilty, each having to pay their own costs.

Now, part of the problem of making history come to life is that the pages of history are silent, but if we turn to the year 1853 we can, for that year, recreate the soundscape of Darsham. That year saw an agricultural census of Suffolk, the statistics of which have survived on the basis of the Hundreds. In our Hundred of Blything there were roughly 65,000 quadruped farm animals, all of which needed food and care. The 3,575 horses needed stables and farriers, the 827 colts had to be trained to be useful. The 2,602 milch cows needed milking and the 1,018 calves needed careful handling. The 17,225 ewes and 20,136 lambs needed shepherding, the 11,001 pigs needed swineherds and the 2,612 'other cattle' may have included more than a few oxen. In all this there was work and sound. The combined noise of 65,000 farm animals, plus dogs and cats, plus geese and poultry, plus the birdsong generated from the then 3,126 acres of woodland and the miles of hedgerows, taken altogether, must have made quite a healthy racket, certainly as each group of animals was either moved or fed.

In effect, our forebears were living in a vast open-air zoo. Into the midst of this soundscape came the railway. The railway put Darsham back on the map when it opened in 1859 — but more of that later.

The agricultural census of 1853 (printed in 'Suffolk in the Nineteenth Century' (1856) by John Glyde pp.341 ff) was based on local returns, but their survival is unlikely. The census gives us a useful picture of the context in which Darsham was operating. In rough terms, out of the total of 91,500 acres in the Hundred, 50,500 acres were under tillage and 29,000 were under grass. The acres under tillage can be split into percentages as follows: 29% Wheat; 27% Barley; 14% Turnips; 12% Beans & Peas; 5% Mangolds; 9% bare fallow and various assorted small crops. The grassland was characterised as: 55% permanent pasture; 27% Clover, Lucerne, etc; 14% sheepwalks and downs and 3% irrigated meadows. Whilst the details of Darsham's agriculture may not be recoverable, our village was part of this overall picture. The agricultural cycle of farmland and livestock was challenging even for the hardy and the strong.

Another part of the background within which Darsham lived was the ongoing difficulties of agriculture. Part of the difficulty was that, from the point of view of the people on the ground, working harder seemed to pay no dividends. In 1834, the High Sheriff of Suffolk had convened a meeting at Ipswich to consider the depressed state of agriculture. The result was a petition to the House of Commons reciting the signatories' "sorrow and alarm, the rapidly increasing difficulties under which they labour, and the utter ruin in which they must speedily and inevitably be involved, unless some of the heavy burthens, under which they struggle are removed, or some increased means of meeting them are afforded...." Over 8,000 farmers, yeomen and others signed the petition.

In 1835, the East Suffolk Society for the Protection of Agriculture, meeting at Framlingham, considered how to respond to "the continued and increasing depression of Agriculture." The Society came to the unanimous resolution: "That the agriculture of the Kingdom being the first of all its concerns, it is essential for the peace, welfare and security of all classes of society, that it should be relieved from its present state of overwhelming distress, by an early and active interposition of Parliament."

These authentic voices from an industry that was struggling for survival can be augmented by the title of a prize essay published by the East Suffolk Agricultural Association in 1845 on the subject: "On the best means of providing employment for Labourers in Agricultural Parishes through the Winter." This was part of the problem — a problem that lingered for years.

This was the era when national history refers to the

Crimean War, the Charge of the Light Brigade, the Indian Mutiny and statesmen such as Disraeli and Palmerston, but we are concerned with local history, not distant greatness. So then, the railway came to Darsham in 1859, forming the last link between Woodbridge and Halesworth to connect London with Lowestoft & Great Yarmouth, bringing considerable trade and distinction to our little village.

Of course, being a railway, there were problems with the line. These are just local incidents — in 1865 a north-bound engine without a train fell off the track about 1¾ miles north of Darsham Station. The track had recently been flooded, the engine was credited with going too fast at 37 m.p.h., and the fastenings on the rails were already regarded as obsolete and dangerous. The engine rolled down the steep embankment and the driver and firemen were both badly scalded. They were taken to Halesworth Hospital where they died some days later

In 1871, the axle of a truck on a south-bound goods train broke about 2 miles north of Darsham Station. But also in 1871, the wife of a gatekeeper at the Middleton level crossing, about ¾ mile south of Darsham Station, whilst opening the gate in the absence of her husband, and in a hurry for a lady who wished to cross the line, was hit and killed by a train.

In 1874, a cart laden with beet was hit by an express train to London whilst crossing the railway line at Darsham. The cart was knocked off the shafts, and the horse ran away, but no-one was injured. Also in 1874, two plate layers returning to the station on a repair trolley were hit by an engine and both were killed. In 1875, the gates of a level crossing between Halesworth and Darsham were run through and broken by a train. The negligence of the gate keeper was blamed. In 1895, a 74 year old railway truck inspector from Ipswich, visiting Darsham Goods Shed, was hit by a train and killed whilst crossing the line. Evidently the mixture of man and machines has always been hazardous!

It was a major achievement that on the opening run in 1859, a train passed from Lowestoft to Ipswich in 1½ hours (curiously this was the same time as the scheduled stopping service in 2006). In 1860, the scheduled journey time from Darsham to Ipswich was 1¼ hours, and from Darsham to London took 4¼ hours. The express from Darsham to London was 35 minutes faster. The 3rd class single fare from London to Darsham was 7s10½d (40p).

The railway which brought such calamity to some people helped to insulate our village against some of the uncertainties when bad times returned. The fifties and sixties were prosperous, but from about 1875 until 1900 arable farming endured an almost continuous series of bad harvests and 1879 was regarded as the worst year. The summer was wet and wheat was still being harvested at the beginning of October. Then there was severe winter weather from the end of November until Christmas. Landlords had to reduce rents and, within a few years, were being advised to let farms at any rent they could obtain. An example of the decline of local prosperity could be taken from the assertion that the rent drawn from Lord Stradbroke's estate in 1895 (J.Thirsk & J.Imray "Suffolk Farming in the Nineteenth Century" [1958] p.30) was only one third of what it had been in 1875. Figures exist (Royal Commission on Agriculture: Report on the County of Suffolk 1895 - Appendix A8) to show that land values in Darsham dropped by 45% from 1873 to 1894. A combination of bad weather, and increasing inefficiency of labour as better workers tended to emigrate, as well as foreign competition, meant that farmers were trapped in an impossible situation. Central and west Suffolk did not have a good railway system through which to deliver their produce. Darsham Station came to our rescue, but difficulties remained.

In the midst of all this gloom, farmers began to feel that the best future for Suffolk farming would lie in the development of dairy farming. Note that in the agricultural census of 1853 there had been surprisingly few milch cows. The industry surrounding these animals was mainly in rearing beef: to every two cows there was one calf, and a cow produces milk for only two thirds of its adult life. A reduction for grazing for beef, and development of new grazing mixtures for dairy animals would be of benefit if a market for milk could be found.

By 1861, the railway network was already delivering more than one million gallons of milk each year to London. By 1871, the figure had grown to around 10 million gallons, but then in 1872, milk cooling apparatus was introduced, and chemical preservatives a few years later. Now milk could be brought to London from Darsham. (P. Atkins: 'The Growth of London's Railway Milk Trade 1845-1914' - Journal of Transport History 1978 No 4 (New series 4) September pp.208-226)

There was a downside. Experienced dairy maids were going to the towns where they could earn a better living. They would not return. In 1874 the average Suffolk weekly wage for a dairy maid was 13s 6d (65p), but by 1893 this had fallen to 12s (60p) (Thirsk & Imray, p.35). There was no great attraction to dwell in Darsham on such a level of pay. To counteract the shortfall of labourers in the dairy farming industry the Eastern Counties Dairy Institute was founded at Akenham in 1888. By 1895 the decision had been made to move into Ipswich, to Gippeswyk Park, in order to attract a potentially larger labour force. It expanded to train a thousand students a year.

Darsham was ahead of the game in all this. We were very fortunate that a Scots farmer came down from

Scotland to take the tenancy of Whitehouse Farm in 1885, hiring a special train to bring with him his family and his entire stock of animals and farm machinery.

James Black was part of a wave of Scottish farmers to leave Scotland and settle in Suffolk and they were among the few people who made Suffolk land pay. Typically, whilst the Scots in Suffolk led a return to dairying they brought a new approach. Some of their land they put down to grass as leys for a few years though they did not attempt to restore permanent pasture. The Scots farmers brought Ayrshire cows and kept them under cover for most of the year. This was a turnaround from the Suffolk practice of the early nineteenth century whereby cows lived out of doors, and were milked in the fields, only being brought into the yard in frost and snow. The Scots fed their herds on hot food, including grain from the breweries. All these changes led to higher yields. Much of their milk production was sent to London (Thirsk & Imray p.36); indeed, James Black sent milk to London by train. Thus the railway proved to be a saviour for farming in Darsham.

Reference has already been made to the colossal amount of writing about Victorian England. In the published series on 'The Agrarian History of England and Wales,' the volume on the period 1850 –1914 (ed E.J.T.Collins, Cambridge, 2000), runs to more than two thousand pages. In the midst of these acres of print, we read in connection

WHITE HOUSE FARM.

James Black and his family
who came down from Scotland
with his Farming Implements and Animals
to farm at Whitehouse Farm in 1885

Darsham Station c.1914

Mr Page of Yoxford with the Shunting Horse

with East Anglian farming: "Dairying resumed in the outlying clay-till parishes of Ipswich, such as Sproughton, or between Norwich & Diss, around Long Stratton, before 1885. It spread sporadically throughout the district, along the railway line of the Great Eastern Railway with collection points at Diss, Haughley and Stowmarket and along the Suffolk coastal line with a depot at Darsham." (p.381-2).

With the development of the sidings, the trucks being moved into place by a shunting horse, facilities at Darsham Station offered a useful freight terminus to other local enterprises. Smythe & Sons of Peasenhall dispatched their seed drills all over England and overseas, starting at Darsham Station. When the new Sibton Church organ arrived for installation in 1872, it came via Darsham Station (the goods label to that effect is still inside the organ case).

Goods were sent and arrived by rail. Coal was now easily, and more cheaply, available and when our line was opened coal could be moved at the rate of three farthings per ton per mile. Such machinery as threshing machines manufactured by Richard Garrett of Leiston since 1815 had been powered by horses, but now cheaper coal meant that steam power could come to farms within the reach of the railway. Garrett's had a good reputation for machinery for when James Laird wrote on English Agriculture in 1851, his chapter on Suffolk included the words: "Nothing can exceed the delicacy and precision of Garrett's horse-hoe, which is looked upon by the farmers of this county as an implement indispensable to clean cultivation." No doubt Garrett's horse-hoes were used on the fields of Darsham. In 1881, it is estimated that the railways delivered 26 million gallons of milk to London. This figure had more than doubled by 1901, and by 1911 reached 80 million gallons. Railway milk was big business, and Darsham had its little share.

Meanwhile, life in Darsham was ruffled by a tragedy at Priory Farm. On Sunday, 15th September, 1867, the farmer, Mr Capon, was woken by a neighbour shouting "Fire!" Mr Capon ran to Yoxford to fetch the fire engine and then had to send for the Garrett's company engine from Leiston. It appears that a young man had got too drunk at the Harvest Supper to go home, and went to sleep in an outhouse apparently with a tobacco pipe. The shed caught alight and poor Frederick Catton, aged 18, perished, along with a fat bullock, a barn and several outbuildings. Mention of Priory Farm recalls the nearby post mill with a two-storey round house which functioned until 1935. Darsham Mill served customers from as far afield as Leiston and Halesworth. The mill accounts book for 1878-79 survives. A sack of flour cost from £1. 8s 0d - £2. 3s 0d; 5 stone of best flour cost from 9s. 0d - 10s. 6d.

The railway was to serve another kind of Mill in Darsham.

The Darsham Windmill

This shows the horses King, Queen, Duke, Duchess and Kitty ready to start the day at Darsham Mill, in 1910.

Photos from East Anglian Magazine - July 1957 & Jan 1959

Darsham's First O.A.Ps 1908

Darsham Post Office pre 1939

In the mid 1860's William Clarke, a miller, had built a Coprolite Mill. This was a steam mill and it stood in the field behind his cottage now called 'Aisthorpe.' in the Street. Coprolite was a hard stoney mass, said to be the fossilised droppings of prehistoric animals. Large deposits had been found in Suffolk & Cambridgeshire and when ground up, proved to be a valuable source of fertilizer particularly for improving grassland. The Darsham Coprolite mill flourished and William Clarke continued to do business for upwards of twenty years, but by the 1880's phosphates were being imported more cheaply from the U.S.A. The business failed, the mill was dismantled, and the storage sheds sold to Mr Martin the local builder.

There was local pride in having a windmill. In the same way there was local pride in having a post & telegraph office. Darsham had had a post office since 1873 and a telegraph office since 1887. In 1898, Darsham had one of only 77 telegraph offices in Suffolk, and was listed as a potential location for a telephone call office. Communication was important. Had Mr Capon been able to phone Yoxford for the fire brigade in 1867 a young man's life might have been saved as well as his barn and fat bullock.

The themes running through this chapter on the nineteenth century in Darsham have been an increase in mechanisation and improvements in agriculture leading to sporadic decreases in poverty for some but also migration from the village — trends which will be seen to have major significance in the final chapter.

Increasing stability was also due to the increased effectiveness of administration (the precedence of parliamentary statute over common law), and with this came pressure for universal franchise, education and the further eradication of poverty through a developing welfare state.

The recorded population figures for Darsham had peaked at 573 in 1831, and had fallen to 342 by 1911. In 1901 it was a matter of some pride that 79 residents had the vote, but also around 1901, a whole day's stone picking would earn a woman or child a mere two shillings.

Parliamentary returns show that in 1880 - 81, Darsham school had places for 85 children, with an average attendance of 43. Strangely, local figures showed an average attendance of 91, which was a very high proportion of the total number of 113 children in the parish aged 4 - 14. The Education Act of 1870 had made education compulsory for all children in this age group.

Children were a feature of village life. With large families there must have been moments when people felt overwhelmed by hordes of irrepressible children. The headmaster of the school at Yoxford called William Busby collected anecdotes featuring children and recorded some of them in a book called '*Hodge Podge*,' published in Halesworth, in 1914. It is appropriate to recall in this way the age of innocence before the Great War when village humour was an antidote to agricultural hardship, and a traditional way of keeping a sense of proportion about village worthies. Thus it was that the vicar repeatedly asked for a lamp for the pulpit in Darsham Church, and for years, no-one would give him one — need one wonder why?

Research suggests that there might have been a Darsham source for some of the material in William Busby's book. Although the stories in the book are unattributed, it is curious that there might have been an extra dimension of local interest. Obviously the classroom question "Whom did Queen Victoria marry?" produced a response that could have come from any local village.

Pupil no 1: "The Prince of Saxe —, Saxe —."
Pupil no 2: (excitedly) " The Prince of Saxmundham."

But there was a Miss Eve Busby who was organist at Darsham Church until 1913, who was the daughter of Mr Busby, at Yoxford. The following story which was included in *Hodge Podge* was not unique to Suffolk, but knowing that this was coming in her father's book could have precipitated Miss Busby's departure from her post at Darsham: It was the custom in a certain village not to begin the service until the Squire arrived, but one Sunday, before his arrival, the Vicar began with the opening sentence, "When the wicked man turneth away" — but he proceeded no further, because the clerk looked up and said: "Sir! Sir! he's not here yet."

However, one story does seem to have a 'local authenticity', it is recorded that in 1909, a cyclists' service was held at Darsham, and the Mayor of Beccles read the lesson. Busby printed the following story, which seems more than a coincidence. " The following incidence occurred one Sunday, on the occasion of the Cyclists' Church Parade:— His Worship, the Mayor of a neighbouring town had promised to read the lessons. Vicar's Warden had been deputed to show His Worship into the Squire's pew and is waiting when a gentleman enters alone, and he is thus addressed by the warden:

Warden: "Do you know whether the Mayor has arrived?"
Gent: "Oh yes, the Mayor has arrived."
Warden; "Is he accompanied by his staff?"
Gent: "Yes."
Warden: "And his officers?"
Gent: "Yes, there are sixteen of us."
Warden: "Then you are his Beadle I suppose?"
Gent: "Oh no, I am the Mayor."

Collapse of warden, and profuse apologies. The warden was told "twas a good job the Mace had been left at home, or he might have been brained on the spot, and his wife thought he was very foolish not to know the Mayor from 'the hub of East Anglia,' although he was dressed as an ordinary mortal." The Vicar's Warden, the Squire, Mr Parry-Crooke, of Darsham House, who was also a Justice of the Peace, might not have welcomed the recital of these stories at his expense! Perhaps Miss Busby simply decided to 'jump' before she was 'pushed'!

We were talking of education. Whilst school indeed became compulsory for children between the ages of 4 - 14 by the Education Act of 1870, parents must have welcomed their children leaving school to add to the family income. The working day was long, especially in the summer with extra hours of daylight, but Darsham had a night school, run by the Vicar and an assistant. 21 adults were on the register intent on continuing self-improvement and raising their chances in life. In addition a 'Technical Carving Class' was held for those who were keen to learn another trade.

The first of January, 1909, was an epic day for the elderly in England. On that day old age pensions became available for those aged 70 or more. Receiving a pension did not carry the stigma of poor relief and this new payment made a huge difference to many folk in very straightened circumstances. The maximum pension of 5 shillings a week was only payable to those whose income was not greater than 12 shillings a week and, initially, only those with no criminal convictions and who had never received support from the Poor Law were eligible. These small payments meant that the country was turning its back on a system which could reduce old age to a penurious misery. It must have been a great joy, for example, to Mr & Mrs Potter of Darsham to have lived to see the introduction of the pension. She died in 1910 aged 87, and when he died in 1914, at the age of 81 he was the oldest pensioner in the village at the time.

However, there was a sting in the tail of the years before the Great War. Researchers in 1913 discovered that whilst the cost of living rose 10% between 1900 and 1910, wages of ordinary labourers rose only 3%. Prices increased a further 5% between 1910 and 1912. The principal investigator, Seebohm Rowntree, concluded that labourers were struggling to survive on insufficient wages. (Pamela Horn: The Changing Countryside in Victorian and Edwardian England and Wales [1984] p.217).

So, the era before the Great War closed, with a precarious prosperity, a whiff of scandal, village humour, and the relentless chuffing of the engines on our railway line.

£846 of FUND RAISING IN DARSHAM 1914 - 1918

British Red Cross	£288. 10s. 0d
Suffolk Prisoner of War	£169. 4s. 0d
Parcels for Darsham Servicemen	£ 78. 11s. 2d
General War Fund	£ 72. 19s. 3d
Farmers Red Cross Fund	£ 69. 19s. 6d
Belgian Relief Fund	£ 26. 19s. 6d
Merchant Seamens' League	£ 25. 13s. 6d
Mission to Seamen	£ 24. 14s. 8d
East Suffolk Hospital	£ 17. 18s. 1d
Sick & Wounded	£ 13. 0s. 0d
East Suffolk War Fund	£ 11. 5s. 0d
Lord Roberts Memorial	£ 5. 10s. 0d
Church Army	£ 5. 5s. 0d
Suffolk Red Cross	£ 4. 16s. 9d
Henham Hospital	£ 4. 12s. 6d
Minesweepers Fund	£ 4. 8s. 6d
War Hospitals Supply Fund	£ 3. 13s. 0d
The Queen's Work for Women	£ 3. 1s. 0d
National Institute for the Blind	£ 3. 0s. 0d
Palestine Relief Fund	£ 2. 8s. 0d
Halesworth Hospital	£ 2. 2s. 0d
British Women's Hospital	£ 2. 2s. 0d
War Hospital Supply Depot	£ 2. 2s. 0d
Y.M.C.A.	£ 2. 0s. 0d
Princess Mary's Fund	£ 1. 13s. 0d
Overseas Club	£ 1. 1s. 0d

Cattleman

WILFRED (Dilly) SHARPE
1924 - 2004

Chapter 9

Keeping Sight of Humanity 1914 - 2000

During this period of history, life in Darsham has changed out of all recognition. Those living at the time of World War I would not recognise life at the end of the millennium. In 1914 an almost feudal system existed where the two estates in the parish employed the majority of the working population who lived in the village. By the end of the century these estates had been broken up and sold and mechanisation has enabled farms to be run almost single handed. The busy village of the pre-1914 era has vanished.

Nearer to our own times we encroach upon living memory, so the need to preserve the privacy of the individual is important by relating only that which is already in the public domain.

The words for the title of this chapter come from a headline in the *Times* of 1st December, 1980, standing over a letter from Darsham resident, Mr Bill Peberdy, but that was from the much later, more comfortable years of the century. It is necessary first to think about Darsham in the Great War. When Mr A.J.Moody died in 1992, we lost our last resident veteran of the First World War.

When war began in August, 1914, it was not long before the Saturday editions of the *Times* announced that the latest war news would appear in special Sunday editions. Clearly people felt as involved then as when they participate in a modern war through television coverage. Darsham was one of the centres from which Sunday editions, delivered by train, could be collected.

News from the War Front was reported in detail in the newspapers of the day along with individual photographs of local soldiers who had been wounded or killed in action but, after the first few months, the reporting of Zeppelin raids and the damage done was severely curtailed. It was not best practice to help the enemy by publishing details of his successes.

Local news unrelated to the war continued as before. For example, in 1915 a 26 year old Darsham born railwayman, Herbert Canham Moore, was killed by a train whilst he was working in the shunting yard at Saxmundham Station. He had been married for just two weeks. Also came the report of the marriage in June 1915 at Darsham Church, of Philip Newby of Halesworth, a Corporal in the 4th Suffolk Regiment. He had just recovered from war wounds received in France. Twelve days later he had to leave to return to the Front.

In Darsham, local fund raising for servicemen proceeded conscientiously and reaped generous giving. Over the four years of the First World War almost £850 was raised in Darsham. This was a huge amount for a such a small parish where so many of the menfolk were away at the front. The war unleashed a process of social change. Locally, this was a long drawn-out affair experienced as the unravelling of a society. Village structures of wealth and authority were slowly dismantled.

This process has been reflected in the way that answers to the question: "What is History?" have changed since the 1914-1918 war. Some people might feel that the years since 1919 are too recent to provide history — except that the focus of history has switched from the doings of the great and good (and the bad) to our common struggles and achievements. The ex-servicemens' hut came to provide a village focus outside the control of the gentry even though they continued to be heavily involved on most of the committees of the village organisations.

The post-war era begins with a graphic illustration of social class division: on Thursday 12th June, 1919, the *Times* carried an advertisement for the sale of Rookery Park, Yoxford, describing the house as having 23 bedroom and dressing rooms, electric light and central heating! This was a world away from the life of local cottagers. In 1924, and in 1927, Darsham School ran out of coal in the bitter winter weather. The school records show local cases of typhoid in 1914 and again in 1923. In 1919, measles reached epidemic proportions with only 18 out of the 72 children in attendance at school. Mrs Parry-Crooke sent a barrow load of coal from Darsham House to rescue the situation on more than one occasion — life could be very hard.

The distinction between the local ethos and 'county' expectations was shown in the way that in the period 1919 - 1936 the *Times* carried various notices of 'situations vacant' at Darsham House, with Mrs Parry-Crooke requiring parlourmaids, housemaids and a cook. She was plainly willing to recruit locally, as indeed she did, and she had a reputation as a good employer, but staff who were going to have significant interaction with guests were perhaps more 'suitable' if they came from further afield with a good reference from another family of the gentry. Meanwhile, the names of Purvis, Parry-Crooke, Rodocanachi and Petrocochino were bracketed with Darsham in the *Times* records of Births, Marriages and Deaths in the inter-war years.

Whilst there were high points as when the Times reported that the ewes of Mr Hugh Hall, of Priory Farm, had done well at a livestock sale in 1930, the inter-war years were generally bad for trade and very hard for many farmers. The names of two people linked to Darsham were listed under the Bankruptcy Acts: Mr C.C.James of the Green (1933) and Mr T.C.O'Nyon of Horwood Lane (1922). In 1938, Herbert Holmes, who farmed at Hinton Hall, was convicted of failing to pay Unemployment and Health

Insurance for two weeks in respect of four of his workers. He said that he had not been able to pay until he received his oat and barley subsidy.

It has been said that "the poor are always with us" and over the 26 years from 1914 - 1940, no fewer than 56 people from Darsham entered the workhouse and of that number at least 15 of them died there.

The number of people living in Darsham have changed drastically — no doubt partly due to the changes in working practices — down from just over 500 in 1841 when families were larger, to 350 just before the First World War; until at the Millennium when the population was approximately 230.

The number of dwellings had increased over the years but most were no longer occupied by families with children. After the Second World War, the older children were bussed to larger schools in Saxmundham and Leiston. Darsham school gradually became unviable until the numbers were down to 12 pupils and the school was closed in 1966.

Between 1928 and 1938, the cost of a Day Return ticket on an excursion train from Darsham to London was between 5s.0d and 5s. 9d. Whether many villagers could afford this was questionable. The newspapers recorded that in 1930 and 1932, the London North Eastern Railway had awarded special prizes to Darsham Station in the Best Kept Station Competition. This was well written up in the Leiston Observer when Mr Stokes, the Station Master, showed the reporter around the waiting room, where the walls displayed the certificates won every year for the past seven years since the competition was started. His staff showed pride in their station and were rewarded for their hard work.

1939 was a strange year for Darsham. A goods train was derailed at Darsham Station in April; at the beginning of September, war was declared on Germany and a group of 36 evacuees with adults arrived from schools in Ilford, Essex. Before the end of September, John Walter Parry-Crooke had died at Darsham House. So 1939 marked the derailment of our traditions of squirarchy and the beginning of a new and damaging war. Darsham folk were taken around the world — technology sprouted out of the ground with the Radar towers at R.A.F. High Street, the radar station recently built up on the Turnpike. Soldiers and equipment were arriving regularly at Darsham Station for training at the battle school towards the coast.

Whether it was from the relief of surviving the war years we cannot know, but conscience had pricked the mind of a visitor to Darsham railway station. The *Leiston Observer,* Saturday, 30th April, 1949, carried the following story:

A Conscience parcel ?

Mr L. Stannard, Stationmaster at Darsham, received a strange "Easter Egg" on Easter Monday. On opening a parcel sent anonymously through the post, he was surprised to find enclosed the book of the New Testament and Psalms which had been missing from the station since October, 1943. Originally presented by the British & Foreign Bible Society to the London & North Eastern Railway Darsham Station, it was, prior to October 1943, always to be found in the Waiting Room. As it has been returned in good condition it has been restored to its rightful home, the Waiting Room.

However here is an account of a rather different sort of egg story - a rotten egg as far as the Yoxford & Darsham Farmers Association Ltd., was concerned.

Darsham had become a hive of activity in the war years; old patterns of authority were shaken off and people rose to assert their new self-consciousness, even challenging central government on this occasion: Darsham achieved a new accolade as it came to figure in the history of constitutional law.

For some years before the war the Yoxford & Darsham Farmers Association Ltd., had run a successful local egg packing and marketing scheme. Eggs collected from local suppliers were presumably, washed, graded, packed, and sold on to local retailers. So successful was the scheme that, when the Ministry of Agriculture developed a national egg-marketing scheme in 1941, the Yoxford & Darsham Farmers Association found them selves paying a new tax. The tax was paid in order to compensate other packers who had lost business under the new scheme.

The Yoxford & Darsham Farmers Association at first acquiesced , but later stopped paying the tax. The Minister of Agriculture had sweeping powers in wartime. The Yoxford & Darsham Farmers Association found that some of their egg suppliers were told to send their eggs to other packers; the loss of business to the Association being equal to the amount of tax they should have been paying. They mounted a legal challenge based on the 1688 Bill of Rights. This declared the levying of taxes for the use of the Crown to be illegal without the authority of Parliament.

The legal challenge went all the way to the Court of Appeal. However it was held finally that under the Emergency Powers (Defence) Act 1939, the Minister of Agriculture had acted properly and that there had been no arbitrary levying of money for the use of the Crown.
The challenge of the Yoxford & Darsham Farmers did not arise out of any lack of patriotism but in the spirit of resentment of centralised interference in local affairs. This case not only figured in books on English Constitutional Law, but was even referred to in a commentary on the Constitution of India! Arbitrary taxation is as serious a constitutional issue as is arbitrary imprisonment. It is to the credit of our local farmers that they were willing to

question these impositions and not merely acquiesce. [2 All ER 38]

The post war period brought the biggest changes to the village. Men who had fought in the War expected to return to better conditions at home. Housing was one of the main immediate requirements but the returning heroes found this still hard to come by. In 1946, the Blything Rural District Council discussed the adaptation of the ex-RAF hutted camp at Haw Wood at Darsham. People were at the end of their tether and squatters had moved in to occupy some of the huts. It meant that the Housing Committee had to do some thing at last and an approach was made to the various ministries in government to release the site.

Like most governmental procedure, nothing moved very quickly. Early in 1947, the *Leiston Observer* carried the story of the latest squatter to take up residence in the huts. It was the 86 year old Mrs Liza Wright, of Halesworth. She said that she was thoroughly enjoying life having lived alone for the past 29 years. Even in the coldest weather she would sit by the open door, head and shoulders draped with a blanket. She had lived a hard life working in the fields for 8 - 10 hours a day picking stones and singling beet. Still in possession of all her faculties, she was able to read a newspaper without the aid of spectacles.

The site was released by the Air Ministry and handed over to the Rural District Council and the huts were partitioned, the electricity, water, and drainage services checked, and eleven families were able to move in. The year 1947 had seen the connection of electricity in almost the whole of the parish. Electricity connection had to be paid for, and the Parish Church needed to raise the necessary £275 by the usual village events. The Vicar, the Revd. H. Ruglys, wrote to the Queen to ask if she would give a donation. A table cloth and glassware was donated by the Queen and a set of tea cups and saucers and goblets from Queen Mary were awarded as prizes at a whist drive.

Further changes came to the village in 1955 when the mains water was brought to the parish from the Walpole pumping station via the new water tower at Heveningham signalling the end of any further outbreaks of typhoid, but Darsham residents had to wait until 1971 for the sewerage to be connected — Darsham had then arrived in the 20th century. The Ex-servicemen gave their hut to the Parish Council in 1953 and the Womens' Institute Hut was amalgamated with it in 1970 - both were milestones in the history of the parish. The linked buildings now form the Village hall. Together with the Church and Chapel, our trio of public buildings enable us to continue village life as it should be lived.

The re-focussing of historical interest to include the local and the particular is illustrated in 1958 when the *Times* carried the news from Hong Kong that the inshore minesweeper H.M.S. Darsham had been involved in the

The tanker collision
at the railway station in 1963

Darsham station staff - 1948

Station Cottages for the Railway Staff

Darsham Station won
many awards in the
Best Kept Station Competitions

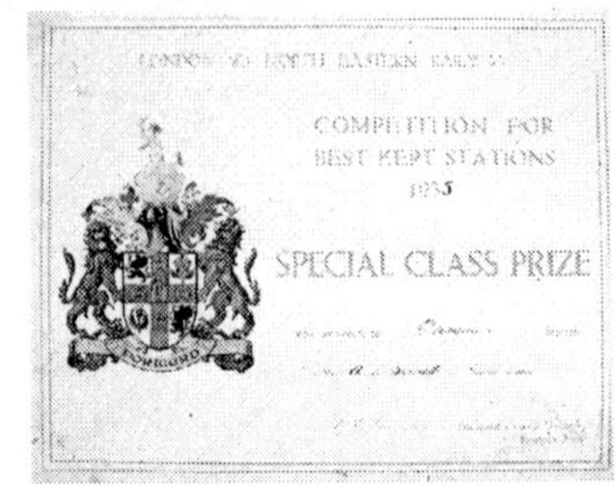

LONDON & NORTH EASTERN RAILWAY

COMPETITION FOR
BEST KEPT STATIONS
1935

SPECIAL CLASS PRIZE

[illegible]

rescue of men and children after a junk was sunk in a collision. This was the same H.M.S. Darsham whose ship's bell was presented to Darsham Parish Council when the ship was de-commissioned in 1965. The little ship and the tall landmark radar towers of Darsham are now no more, but the ship's bell and badge and one of the red lights from the very top of one of the towers are now back in the village, both truly tangible reminders of wartime Darsham.

The readiness to recount personal stories and opinions gave a new dimension to the nation's view of itself. So, on Thursday, 13th June, 1963, when a coach taking old folk from Essex on their annual outing to the seaside collided with a petrol tanker, right on the Darsham level crossing, the words of one elderly lady passenger were printed for *Times* readers throughout the world: "This has given me something to talk about for the rest of my life. It has been the most exciting day of my 84 years."

Later that same year, on Friday, 13th December, Darsham made a splash once again in the news when the report came that a Lowestoft based trawler, the Loch Lorgan, had run aground in rough seas and high winds off Great Yarmouth. Twice the boat had almost capsized and the life rafts swept overboard. The seven-man crew, with their Chief Engineer, Mr Colin Nunn of Station Cottages, Darsham, was rescued by the Caister lifeboat. When it was found that the trawler had righted itself, the crew set out again on the lifeboat to board the trawler only to find it aground once more on the north beach at Yarmouth — A story that must have given Mr Nunn something to talk about for many years!

In 1995, the Darsham Women's Institute was 75 years old. An occasional theme of talks given by their invited speakers right from their first annual programme was Suffolk History — showing that there has long been a thirst to appreciate our past. Historical talks included 'Suffolk Dialect' (1933), 'Dunwich' (Mr Stanley Godfrey of the Barne Arms, Dunwich - 1945), 'Darsham & Westleton' (1979). Our interest and affection for the past became a source of strength and stability as the pace of social change accelerated towards the end of the century.

An unexpected note of appreciation of a much cherished local facility came in an article in the *Times* in 1993 complaining that people liked gazing out of a train window and that trains were going too fast to see anything properly. President Mitterrand of France had poked fun at the slow-speed channel rail-link. But this article concluded :—

> "How about Darsham, on the East Suffolk line. It is now an unmanned halt, but at least no TGV rushes through to disturb the rural calm. Try it President Mitterrand."

It is uncertain when computers arrived in Darsham. The effects of computers can be illustrated by a letter from Mrs

Sara Low of Darsham House, to the *Times* in 1998:—

> "Sir, I was somewhat surprised to receive a letter from the Royal Bank of Scotland, addressed to my husband who died late last year. This in itself is not a surprise as it takes a certain amount of time for news to trickle through .... The odd thing about this letter is that it is addressed to "Mr Peter Low Deceased" both on the letter itself as well as on the envelope ..... I am quite concerned that the computer has not yet learned that deceased means dead."

In a *Times* article published the day before Remembrance Day in 1998, a distinguished local author, Libby Purves, wrote about her visit to the battlefields of Italy with our elderly parishioner Dilly Sharpe. She wrote:— "Before he was 20, he saw death and despair and triumph, judged officers and men against lurid horror, marched through the heart of Europe and into history. When his country had finished with Dilly, it gave him a suit, a pair of shoes, a hat, a raincoat, and a rail warrant home to Darsham. He walked home from the station, and his mother got his tea, and that was the end of Dilly's war." Libby's concluding words might act as a prelude to the end of this short book:— "A curtain of understanding and expectation, usually impenetrable, has fallen between the generations. We were glad, over those few days to have that curtain raised."

One may hope that this book will have a similar function. History does not stop at the Millennium. Happily in 2000 we still had a pub, a railway station, one could hire a bicycle at Byways Bicycles in Priory Lane, we could still buy our petrol at the Station Garage complex where a small shop served locals and the travelling public alike. We still held our annual village fete. We can still celebrate past and present national events. But within the time scale of this last chapter, we have lost the cricket club, the football team, the quoits team — the sports of yesteryear, which interacted with other local villages. With a predominantly older population our carpet bowls team now holds it own in the area competitions, hearts and minds are occupied by a weekly 'keep fit' class, and a bi-annual 'craft day.'

So the village itself is gradually changing. We have some new houses, some older cottages are already holiday homes or second homes. We still have the feeling of local opinion and practice in the face of central and remote authority. Our Parish Council has beavered away for an entire century, trying to give a local independent voice.

We still cherish the identity of Darsham contained in its 'planning envelope,' with its 'conservation area,' its church and chapel and village hall.

The School

The Village Hall

Darsham Radar Pylons

Reminders of W.W.II

A light from the top
Of one of the pylons

H. M. S. DARSHAM

CONCLUSION

In Ernest Martin's book 'The Secret People,' he traced English Village Life after 1750. Writing in 1954, he thought that "the village has reached a point when transformations are bound to occur" (p.33). Those changes certainly have come upon us, and some suspect that the process of change is now accelerating, but it is Martin's very first paragraph to which we should pay special attention:—

"Someone has defined the village community as a memory of the past and a hope for the future. Because it is both these things, there is a need to see it as a whole — to confront the planners' vision, the urge towards innovation, with the legitimate restraints of custom. Unlike the town, the village has its basis of meaningful tradition, its secret identity, stretching back to the beginnings of soil cultivation."

Thank you for journeying with us through the scattered evidences of history and exploring that secret identity. There are many more stories to tell from the past of Darsham. The extraordinary richness of our archives in this country continues to reveal fresh information about Darsham as more material becomes available on the world wide web. At present there is considerable concern about the backlog in cataloguing archived deposits throughout the country. Future searches will reveal more information about Darsham, but we are confident that all this extra material will fit in with the patterns that we have drawn.

Martin linked memory and hope. The achievements of our forebears in struggling through all that they had to endure should sow the seeds of hope and courage for the future. Altogether history can be quite exciting.

LIST OF PERSONS TAKING CHILDREN OUT OF THE HOUSE OF INDUSTRY 1760 - 1792

S.R.O.Ref: FC65/G1/1

Parishes were responsible for the upkeep of their own paupers in the House of Industry. Each year the parish was required to take at least one pauper out of the House and to allocate that person, sometimes by ballot, to a local employer who would receive £5 from the Parish Poor Rate.
Below is a list of Darsham people taken from the Blything Workhouse.

			Child's Name
1760	Mr James PEAD	took	John HARRIS
1760	Admiral PURVIS		Walter SNELL
1762	Thomas EDMUNDS		John BOYTON
1762	Samuel STEAGEL		.... LODGE
1762	John TEABOLD		.... LODGE
1763	Revd.Buxton *Vicar of Darsham 1748 - 1775*		Martha HARRIS
1764	John SAWING		Ann SNELL
1764	Joseph MILLS		Ann HARRIS *for John Martin's Farm*
1765	Thomas COOPER		John Watling
1768	John COLE		John PLANT *aged 9*
1768	Walter SNELL		Mary PENNY *aged 12*
1769	Widow of John SAWING *(Lydia SAWING)*		Sarah HARRIS
1771	William FIELD		George CATCHPOLE *aged 11*
1772	John WATTS		William LODGE *aged12*
1774	Thomas SKEET		.... ALDRED
1777	James PEAD		Susanna PENNY *aged 13*
1778	Charles PURVIS		Sarah TOOK *aged 13*
10 Oct 1792	Samuel EASTAUGH		Mercy ALDRED
10 Oct 1792	Mr SCARFF		Sarah ALDRED *aged 13*

DARSHAM PEOPLE WHO DIED IN BLYTHING WORKHOUSE 1766 - 1835

All admitted from Darsham

S.R.O.Ref: ADA1/CB1/1

Adm Date	Name	Age	Discharged on Death
4 Jul 1774	Elizabeth BENSTEAD	71	11 Jan 1775 Died
26 Aug 1802	Judith BLOWERS -	19	Oct 1802 Died
13 Jul 1810	John BLOWERS	60	19 Jul 1809 Died
16 May 1814	George BOTWRIGHT	82	15 Apr 1815 Died
11 Oct 1813	John BUCK	71	12 Sep 1814 Died
22 Jan 1810	Sarah BUCK	48	16 Apr 1812 Died
6 Oct 1766	John COLEMAN	7	7 Jun 1767 Died
4 Jul 1808	Mary EVES	74	1 Feb 1809 Died
3 Jul 1797	Elizabeth GODDARD	26	22 Sep 1797 Died
15 Apr 1782	Robert GOODWIN	70	17 Jun 1782 Died
6 Oct 1766	Elizabeth IVES	63	10 Mar 1769 Died
5 Jan 1826	Samuel KERRIDGE	50	12 Apr 1830 Died
20 Jan 1794	Elizabeth LEADER	7	8 Apr 1794 Died
8 Nov 1784	Elizabeth LEEDER	1	16 Nov 1784 Died
15 Apr 1793	Robert NICHOLS	73	21 May 1793 Died
3 May 1802	Benjamin PAGE	59	16 Mar 1803 Died
14 Oct 1822	William PARNELL	70	26 Jun 1824 Died
18 Nov 1816	Sarah PARNELL	1yr 8mo	6 Jun 1817 Died
5 May 1817	MaryAnn PARNELL	Bn in Ho	10 Mar 1818 Died
14 Oct 1822	Sarah PARNELL	72	20 Aug 1823 Died
12 Sep 1774	Henry PENNY	49	28 Oct 1774 Died
00 Jan 1767	Bether PENNY	3mos	19 Apr 1767 Died
16 Jul 1798	Haward SEAMANS	1yr 1mo	12 Jun 1799 Died
14 Apr 1777	John SHADE	80	31 May 1777 Died
14 Apr 1777	Elizabeth SHADE	29	26 Aug 1777 Died
5 May 1800	Hannah STAFF	Bn in Ho	16 Dec 1800 Died
12 Dec 1785	William STARKEY	8	22 Dec 1788 Died
12 Dec 1785	Sarah STARKEY	10	20 Feb 1786 Died
12 Dec 1785	Mary STARKEY	9	28 Mar 1790 Died
9 Sep 1793	William STRINGER	60	4 Apr 1794 Died
30 Nov 1807	Barnabus THURLOW	46	28 Feb 1821 Died
30 Nov 1807	Mary THURLOW	10mo	21 Dec 1808 Died
26 Jan 1784	William TOOK	Bn in Ho	18 Mar 1785 Died
24 Sep 1770	Mary TURNER	70	31 Jul 1771 Died
6 May 1802	John UTTING	62	29 Jun 1802 Died
14 Mar 1785	William WALKER	68	11 Apr 1785 Died
8 Aug 1814	Susan WATLING	92	1 Jan 1815 Died
16 Apr 1781	Elizabeth WATLING	68	11 Mar 1782 Died
28 Sep 1795	James WHITE	2	10 May 1800 Died

NATIONAL FARM SURVEY for DARSHAM - 1941

PRO Ref:
MAF32/882/24

FARM	OWNER/OCC.	YRS.	LABOUR	CATTLE	SHEEP	PIGS	POULTRY	HORSES
Home Farm	Mr E. Cordle	16	4	30	-	13	52	3
Green Farm	Mr E. J. Elmy	8	3	24 -	-	-	240	5
White House Fm & Brakes Lane Frm	Mr C.H.Fairs	20	6	43	5	47	240	5
North End Fm	Mr R.C.Seaman	7mos	-	-	1Ram	-	-	-
Priory Farm	Mr H.R.Hall	19	4	10	244	11	124	9
High Street	Mr J.W.Mayhew [1¼ac]	-	-	-	-	-	30	-
Darsham Hall Fm	J.W.Rickeard	10	11	36	67	93	71	10
Hill Farm	A.W.Robinson	17	-	5	8	1	14	-
Low Farm	Mr A.J.Rodocanachi	13½	6	88	108	-	-	10
Mill Hill Farm	Mr R.G.Searle	2½	4	43	-	4	36	5
Woodbine Cottage	Mr C.W.E.Youell [2½ac]	13	-	-	-	4	66	-

GENERAL OCCUPATIONS in Darsham DURING THE CENSUS YEARS 1841-1901 incl.

Directly involved in Agriculture:

- Farmer
- Bailiff/Steward
- Gamekeeper
- Shepherd
- Horseman
- Carter
- Agricultural labourer
- Timber Carter
- Market Gardener
- Threshing Machine Owner
- Agricultural machinist
- Dairywoman
- Stockman
- Warrener
- Vermin destroyer
- Miller

Indoor Service

- Housekeeper
- Governess
- Nursemaid
- Cook
- Ladies Maid
- Parlourmaid
- Housemaid
- Kitchen Maid

Outdoor Service

- Gardener
- Groom
- Ostler
- Coachman
- Cowboy

Self Employed & Tradesmen

- Blacksmith
- Shoeing Smith
- Miller
- Wheelwright
- Boot & Shoemkr
- Shoe Binder
- Builder
- Carpenter
- Bricklayer
- Undertaker
- Carrier
- Coal Carter
- Maltster
- Woodman
- Hoop & Hurdle Mkr
- Warrener
- Rat & Mole Catcher
- Colt Breaker
- Fisherman
- Tailoress
- Dressmaker
- Corn & Coal Merch
- Landscape Artist
- Boarding House kpr
- Charwoman
- Fish Dealer
- Laundress
- Chimney Sweep
- Tailor

Public Services

- Vicar
- Grocer & Draper
- Shopkeeper/Furniture Broker
- Innkeeper/Publican
- Licensed Brewer
- Postmaster
- Letter carrier/Postman
- P. O. Messenger
- Telegraph Clerk
- Roadman
- Midwife
- Schoolmaster
- Schoolmistress
- Railway:—
  - Station Master
  - Booking Clerk
  - Goods Clerk
  - Signalman
  - Porter
  - Platelayer
  - Gatekeeper
  - General Labourer